HEROINES

AN ANTHOLOGY OF SHORT FICTION AND POETRY

VOLUME 3

Sarah Nicholson & Caitlin White

Editors

I0589719

THE NEO PERENNIAL PRESS

Published by The Neo Perennial Press

Wollongong, Australia.

www.theneoperennialpress.com

Cover design: Tim Donnelly

National Library of Australia Cataloguing-in-Publication entry

Creator: Sarah Nicholson & Caitlin White

Title: Heroines: An anthology of short fiction and poetry. Volume 3/Edited by Sarah Nicholson and Caitlin White.

ISBN: 78-0-9946453-5-7

Subjects: Women--Fiction. Mythology. Fairytale. Folklore

Contents

Medusa's Daughter

I.
our mother sounded like the weather
her voice a grey sky growing dark in the promise of rain
so I am told

her neck was strong, determined
when broken by death it released the storm brewing in her throat
it rained for days, torrents sea-heavy and full from carrying all the
advice
she could no longer give to me

the earth drank it up, lips all muddy with swollen dirt
churning a new ground, a new life
my mother's last act was planting
her handiwork sprouting up in serpents turning through the soil
a message for her daughter

I can see drops of my mother in the long grass
the old sandpit, the woodpile, the rafters
her armour shining like rainbows in oil
she raises her head to the sun, heaving her body to the sky
with a strength that's older than any type of permission

I keep my distance
watching on from the firetrail, the verandah, by torchlight
she moves with everything she has, rib by rib
carving her path in grace
this confidence so easily feared
the legend runs down her spine, down a body like ours:
feared, adored, tired of finding the sun in secret

I like to think she in the long grass is a loose strand of mother's hair
unbrushed fury
a reminder that gorgan is just another word for a woman who cannot
be broken
a woman who died a stepping stone for her daughter and the next
even in death her skin still hummed with a power that was the envy
of man
and envy be the curse that Athena tried to break

in the long grass I find a snake skin
I lift the treasure gentle into the light
all those scales like stepping stones from mother

II.
I do not know what mother is
I know the spit slick mouths of asps and the salt-crusted bite of the
aegean
I know granite face and gorgon pupil
and I know spice covered hands working the marblewood chopping
boards
warm cracked skin like the edge of the basin in drought

but I do not know mother
in the way that the fields of Demeter know mother
yielding and unyielding

my mother keeps her secrets cradled tightly to her stomach;
stories of men and monsters buried in her diaphragm
my mother does not know her mother's secrets
and now that legacy with no head nor tail nor skin is mine

so I want to know grandmother
find mother through her
trace her veins back through ancestry after ancestry
check each lantana choked temple for its rapes
of the before women, of the before medusas
of the women laid on stone tablet after stone tablet

and had no praises slither from their hair
the mothers with no brave legends left to tell their daughters
no python skin hand me downs, only gravestone faces

I want to feel the weight of that legacy settle in my belly
warm and potent, like giving birth
like knowing mother

III.
our mother dreamed us before we came
woke sweating from nightmares of wailing cyclops
babes missing limbs and voices
was handed us whole one after the other
named us virgin, beauty, gift, thunder
was left bloodsoaked and bone-weak
we ripped her flesh open
screaming ourselves into the world and took her strength inside us
left her with less each time

I imagine my mother shrieking her blood to the sky
her body a traitor, no longer hers but ours
echoing pain to the mountains
I imagine this and I wake
screaming myself into the world
I wake and remember I am woman, monster, labyrinth

each and every moon we carry cupfuls of sacrifice
bleaching cotton and concrete in tiny ovals
and count ourselves lucky for the inconvenience
for the absence of growth, of life
this visceral shedding, this gift of no gift at all
we are praised as lifebringers but we walk with death inside us

for every nameless hero who comes to conquer me
I pray Aphrodite not to bless me, to look elsewhere
lay her hands on another's soft belly and leave mine empty
I would make this labyrinth a fortress

line the walls with pitch and flame and burn anything that tried to
grow
but I still have to live here

so I'll make this fortress a garden
will be maiden and crone but not mother to my own
ask Clotho to spin me a different fate
rewrite the prophecy of motherhood
and make it something for which I need only my hands

I'll weave a nest from gum leaves and lavender and nurture it with
lifeblood
pour cupfuls of celebration back into my circle
shed my years like snakeskin
rebirth myself each season into what Medusa could have been

IV.
I am hovering between eagerness and uncertainty / a Persephone:
one foot in the Underworld, the other in the Spring / my old
snakeskin catches in flecks to the new / unsure and afraid / I hide
my blood in cups, bury them beneath the wattle tree / burn with
shame / my mother's ghost skims her fingertips across my cheek—
says nothing / sighs into sunlight and memory / I learn the art of
growing up is to make myself small / press my body into yes, my
heart into quiet / glide a hollow smile of candied teeth and seashells
/ I learn to keep pretense in my pockets / define myself like a
cheekbone / skim over the little lies (I'm fine, how are you?) / I bury
myself in my own body / every look an exhumation, every touch a
desecration / and when my blood comes I am toothfuls of guilt of
relief / oceans of shame of this mess I create / this body quivers / a
fever of stingrays battling for stillness / unsure of itself—myself / a
self stitched together with glass and morning dew / what does it
mean to be a body / what does it mean to be a body that bleeds /
what am I if not this bleeding body / as the first rays of sun skim
across the Aegean my mother's ghost makes baklava / threads
honey, lemon, history with cinnamon, breath, patience / when I ask
her what I am she leads me out to the garden / kneels beside me
beneath the wattle tree / rests her hands atop mine and presses our

fingers into the cool earth / and I am fear and shame and—I am the wattle, just blooming / I am the stained-glass windows above Athena's altar / I am the earth that gives and takes away / I am the tide, rushing in / I am the echo of my mother's spine: a column of stone and sea-glass and rabbit-heart bravery / I am the Library of Alexandria, the city of Carthage, the Garden of Hesperides / and I am burning, burning, burning / I am Cerberus, hound of the Underworld and I will eat you / I am the warmth of my hands, the blade of my tongue / I am the blood that blooms in my belly / leaves crimson poppies on the sheets and down my thighs / leaves me overflowing red, both life and death, and does not ask forgiveness / I am I am I am I am I—release my fingers from the earth and go back inside / In the kitchen, I spill the baklava down my chin, drip it into my lap / the honey slips between my thighs, pools with my blood / I cup it in my hands / an offering / my mother's ghost blesses it with pistachios and perseverance / says, take your time / I unhinge my jaw and birth infinite possibilities / monster and maiden / ask me what I am and I will say: melliferous / blood and honey / weapon and shield / alive and unashamed /

say riot / rest / repeat / remember
take your time.

Baba Yaga, Bony Leg
Brenna Gautam

For months, it seemed everyone knew about the cannibal living in
the birch forest behind our house, but no one would acknowledge it.
When we first moved in, the property surveyor guided my
stepmother by her elbow to the shade of our porch and produced a
nicotine-stained map. He traced the line of demarcation that would
separate our property from the cannibal's with his pinky finger.
"Cannibal, you said?"
"людоед."
My stepmother nodded slowly, eyes roving the tree line, then
thanked the surveyor politely for his services. She was brilliant and
could have been an army interrogator if she'd wanted to, but she
preferred not to ask leading questions. She took long pauses between
thoughts and when she did choose to speak, her sentences were
direct and unflowery, which I imagined made her lectures fantastic.
At the time, she was on sabbatical from her position as Professor of
Toxicology at Saint Petersburg State University, laboring through the
beginning months of an unwanted pregnancy and screaming into
her fist every other night.
(Later, in the garden, I would find four needles pushed so deep into
the mottled skin of a cucumber that only the silver eyes protruded.
"An outlet, Vasilisa. Would you prefer I stab myself? Please bring the
dill and horseradish.")
The property surveyor couldn't accept her signature on the deed, so
we waited until the last rusty streaks of twilight scraped across the
horizon. For the cold to settle in, for the man of the house to arrive.
Then we spent the next six months playacting a script of our lives
where the cannibal didn't exist.
Or, when absolutely necessary, we dealt with it in the strain of
humor characteristic of our motherland. Startled by a distant volley
of fireworks on New Year's Eve, or the mournful swoop of military
planes overhead, my father would faux lament: Must be our pesky
neighbor again. Ignoring my stepmother and stepsister Tanya, he
watched me out of the corner of his eye to see if I'd smile at his little
joke.

At night, I took to locking my bedroom door and dreaming of business school in some faraway land.

"It's a hazard," my stepmother snapped. "What happens if there's a fire?"

"I'll pull myself up and out the window."

As I said this, I exposed the scrawny area of my arm where a bicep should be. (Attempted humor, to make her smile). She expertly flicked an obstinate shard of eggshell off a hardboiled egg and murmured something about how I'd probably choose to self-immolate anyway, just to be with my mother.

I couldn't make her smile anymore. The bleak countryside, dying livestock, percussive pain radiating in cold hammers through her belly. Little crab claw bruises left in her flesh after my father—not wanting to cause a miscarriage or blemish her face—pinched the underbelly of her arms. With her graceful neck and encyclopedic knowledge of forensics, I knew she belonged in a sunlit lecture hall somewhere in Paris or Copenhagen, but her life hadn't turned out that way. And after my new half-sister's birth, the violence metastasized.

My stepmother named the baby Mara, from a bible story about a desert fountain with water so bitter the Israelites could not drink from it. At first, I thought the name carried in its brief syllables a talisman—to keep the thirsty hordes away—but soon realized that little Mara, with her shiny red face and piercing cries, was only adding to the besieged slope of my stepmother's shoulders. And that perhaps the name was just another curse, vindictive, a parent's resignation that some Moses would eventually toss a plank of wood into their daughter's well, forcing the water below to sweeten, that his people may drink, and that perhaps there could be no other namesake for a child born into such a home besides sorrow, bitterness. Tangerine bottles with white caps began populating the bathroom counter.

One evening, every light in our house blinked off simultaneously, like a magician's hat trick, and my father instructed me to ask our neighbor with the generator for some specific batteries and, if possible, a spare flashlight.

"For the love of Christ, enough with the excuses," he sighed (this after I tried to point out the absurdity of asking a cannibal for

7

batteries during a power outage). My stepmother, inscrutable as ever, pretended to have no knowledge of such a thing. So, I hid a fillet knife in the sleeve of my parka and crossed our property line in the dusky forest, keeping my eyes trained on the ground. And despite my transient suicidal ideations, despite complicated feelings towards my father—half revulsion, half frustrating, filial longing for approval—and despite that slow leviathan of survivor's guilt, silently gulping down memories of my mother, I realized I didn't want to be eaten. As I stepped under a gate made of dismembered human legs, with sawed-off hands for bolts and a gaping mouth for a lock, the beginnings of an unalloyed fear bled into the corners of my vision, almost welcome in its simplicity. Past the gate, the birches thinned, and a dozen lampposts lining a driveway seemingly designed for limousine entrances appeared, leading to the cannibal's house.

There, just outside the front door, an emaciated figure with a long nose stood in a dark bathtub, smoking what looked like a fat cigar. As I continued down the driveway, I noticed they weren't really lampposts, but misshapen skulls fastened to the top of cedarwood poles with some translucent, gummy material, tea candles burning in the jawbones like nightmare tiki torches. And the old woman was smoking in a giant mortar, not a bathtub. A huge pestle made of dark granite lay on the ground beside her.

"Another trespasser! Nothing keeps you away, huh? Welcome to the House of Baba Yaga…"

With a grunt, the woman bent down to tap the cigar against the side of her mortar, then heaved herself back upright and rustled the folds of her burlap skirt. Ash floated dreamily into the snow. For a moment, I thought she would hike the coarse material up above her waist and flash me, but she only raised the hem high enough to proffer a gaunt, wasted leg, so malnourished that the muscles had atrophied from the shin bone. It reminded me of the crippled leg of a classmate who used to lie and tell us girls he had stepped on a landmine. Pitiful attempts at flirting and second-hand embarrassment. Nauseated and shaken, I tried not to stare, but every other place I cast my eyes was a tangled mash of knuckles, congealed blood, barbed wire, snowdrift.

I knew Baba Yaga. Of course I knew her. Baba Yaya, Bony Leg. An old woman the government had charged with arson, desecration of cemetery and corpse, murder (felony and first degree), and various other violations of human rights. But she had never been apprehended, and over time, the outstanding charges and wanted posters papering Moscow's urban parks had birthed a cult following that was small and resilient, like the kernel of an apricot, and composed mostly of artists, anarchists, and other nonconformists. Rarely photographed and difficult to biographize, these fans had transformed her into a figure like Rasputin, straddling a slim gold thread between mythos and reality, politics and magic.

It was as if the parts of my body had splintered off into wholly disconnected systems: my heart pounded, but my breath caught. My amygdala tapped out a distress signal to run, run, run, but beneath the taiga, my heels sprouted icicle roots.

"Please don't hurt me," I finally croaked, fully prepared to mount a babbling plea for a chance at some happier rendition of my current life. "I don't have any money, but I'll do anything you want. I can help clean your house, run errands, make a schedule…I can cook omelets for you…."

With a smirk, Baba Yaga told me that she was the most powerful entity I'd ever meet, and that a powerful woman like her had no need for a scheduler or an omelet.

"Even if you became a czarina and traveled the world, meeting important diplomats and generals, you'd still never meet someone as powerful as me."

"If you're so powerful, why do you live out here in the middle of nowhere? Why is your nose so long?"

I didn't mean to be hurtful—and certainly wasn't brave—but adrenalin and cold lungs had morphed my personality into a brash, quilled version of Vasilisa that might slip a knife into someone's liver.

"Ha! Did you know that men have written whole epics about my nose? It's true. They're obsessed with my nose, my leg, my buttocks. How old are you? You're not even a woman yet. I eat noses like yours for breakfast."

In marketing, they called the tactic puffery. The best response is to let someone run out of steam naturally, so I let Baba Yaga continue on like this without comment until she confessed that she wasn't very hungry and could use some company. She was preparing for a long journey south, to Mongolia, and told me that she didn't like packing in silence because her mind always seemed to wander to melancholy territory: glaciers she would never see, disappearing species, wonders of the world sinking into the ocean or collapsing into sediment.

"If you don't mind the mess," she added, surprisingly humble. I could barely believe my luck.

"Oh my gosh, no problem at all. I have a five-year-old stepsister and a newborn halfsister. My life is nothing but mess, believe me."

But hers was messier.

There was simply no meaningful barrier between indoors and out. Squirrels and chipmunks scurried across warped floorboards from room to room, and sharp chicken bones littered the floor. In the toilet room, a swan floated in the bathtub and surprising pops of thistles had sprouted up from the corner of the sink. Magenta against cracked ceramic. The air smelled of cat urine and marijuana. Without her mortar and pestle, Baba Yaga's steps were so jerky and offkilter that I asked whether she would like to lean on my shoulder, but she waved me off, explaining that the Ministry of Defense had invented new technology to identify individuals by their gaits and she was practicing new methods of movement to throw them off her trail. For years afterwards, I would remain aware of the soles of my feet as they connected with the vibrating ground.

Packing consisted of throwing strange items—shortbread cookies, crucifixes, shards of sea glass—into an ugly black suitcase. Still unsure of whether she might turn on me at any moment, I tried to be as helpful as possible. I listened attentively to her instructions on how to balance the luggage. Heavier items in the corners, nothing with talons on the bottom. We spent hours scouring the house for her travel set of razor blades.

Over dinner, Baba Yaga gossiped about her in-laws. I nodded along out of ingrained manners, fatigue, and a burgeoning hope that by the morning, I might be returned to my old life unconsumed.

"I suppose they're actually my ex-in-laws. I keep in touch only to wish them misfortune on their birthdays! Now you see why."

"What about your ex-husband?"

"Dead. Vulture food."

"Oh gosh. I'm so sorry...I didn't know."

"Don't be sorry. He was an ass. He died two weeks before I could kill him."

Ah.

"Don't look so concerned! He tried to poison me too. He took after his father that way. We used to fight like animals. One time he called me a condom."

I truly couldn't fathom a safe response to this, so I just made a show of chewing on my tough chicken, corralling mashed potatoes into a corner of the plate with my thumb.

I finally asked Baba Yaga, "Is it normal for a father to call their daughter a whore, блядь?"

"You shouldn't swear at a kid."

"Oh, gotcha. But that specific swear word—whore—do you think it's a weird thing for a father to say?"

"How would I know? I have no father. I was born from a potato!"

She crossed her eyes and licked mashed potatoes off her plate to make me laugh.

"But if I did have a father," she said, soberly now, looking me straight in the eye, "and he called me блядь. I would definitely kill him. And probably eat him."

For a woman with so much pride in the contours of her wizened figure, I noticed over the course of dinner that she maintained strange eating habits. She preferred the flavorless stalks of broccoli, disposing of the tender florets in a steaming compost heap in her backyard. She enjoyed chicken with the feathers still attached. Her hair was a matted nest of putrid locks and ancient yarn, but she took great pleasure in shaving her legs, championing the sensation of smooth skin against satin sheets.

After dessert, she beckoned me outside to her garden, to watch her son ride his flying chariot. Squinting my eyes against the dark, unable to process all the other impossibilities, what struck me the most was how low the chariot flew. It seemed reckless, the way the carriage wheels and horse hooves nearly clipped the rose bushes. He flew so low to the garden, it seemed like a threat. He flew so near I could see he was faceless, and that his hands shook with violent tremors as they gripped the chariot reigns. Although the sunken place where his face should have been was a velvety black hole, I realized he might nevertheless be looking directly at me, and the thought left me feeling suddenly naked and terrified.

"You were scared," Baba Yaga noted, after the chariot finally ascended a little and disappeared over the crest of a dark hill. "Why?"

I shrugged, hoping to register as nonchalant when in truth, I was still too terrified to speak.

For a long moment, I felt her staring at me in the dark, over the long expanse of her nose.

"Here, stand in my mortar."

Using the pestle as a sort of navigation stick, we stood in her mortar and zoomed across the midnight forest floor, without scarves, wind wrecking our hair, screaming in excitement and terror, leaving a trail of trampled underbrush and smashed mushrooms in our wake. In the mortar, Baba Yaga's body pressed so close to mine that I eventually relaxed and leaned forwards into the back of her warm neck to inhale her sweet, mossy scent. I wrapped my arms around her so fiercely that the insides of my elbows started to ache, and tears froze on my cheeks.

When we returned home, Baba Yaga sat me down in front of her brick stove and began braiding scraps of fabric into my hair. She asked about each of my family members, politely committing their names to memory as we went: "And your stepsister, Tanya, what does she think about it?" Or, "And how long since you last visited Dima's?" The familiar conversation and warmth from the stove lulled me into a happy stupor, but eventually, I began catching myself repeating the phrase "all things considered."

All things considered; it wasn't as bad as it might be. I was saving money to leave home and study marketing in North America, to learn how to charm and manipulate people into investing in important products that might save the world. Perhaps a rune to heal my stepmother's pain. Or a ship to ferry little Mara away from all this. Although, all things considered, it wasn't so bad. I imagined my father didn't act half as often as an urge might sprout, and even when he did, he satisfied himself with glances and grazes. If you think about it, isn't that something to be rewarded? All things considered, isn't having a forbidden desire and ignoring it more commendable than not having the desire at all? Lots of people have odd desires.

For example, a woman named Eirka LaBrie had married the Eiffel Tower.

"The Eiffel Tower is made of wrought iron," Baba Yaga pointed out, "and you are a human."

"I know, but I'm talking about the woman, Erika LaBrie, Mrs. Eiffel. She was attracted to this--"

"Object, yes, I know," she snapped, "you already said that." I could tell she was angry.

"Are you going to cook me?" I asked, but she had already stomped out of the room in a flurry of hops and limps.

The next morning, I woke to find that Baba Yaga had left me a package of batteries, a sack of shortbread cookies, and a skull with a candle inside to guide me through any shadowy parts of the forest between her house and ours. She wasn't in the habit of keeping things in cages, so I shouldn't have been surprised that the brief goodbye note on the table was celebratory rather than sorrowful: Sorry about the early night last night. Needed to rest before the trip! If you need me, I'll be backpacking in Mongolia. Xx, Baba.

At home, the fire from her skull quickly consumed the west facing side of our house.

Angry scorch mark where my stepmother had cowered against the wall.

Blistered remains of my father.

"She gets to sleep in? Meanwhile I've been watching these two all damn morning," my father had explained, not weighing his last words, eyes melancholy and crusty around the corners. "Strange looking lamp. Give it here, I'll show it to her."

He had locked their bedroom door behind him, of course.

My sisters and I screamed and wailed until our throats were collectively shredded, and the remaining shreds were ruined anyway by acrid smoke that filled the old structure from cellar to attic, staining everything the color of a graveyard.

That night, I shaved my legs with a half-melted razor. I wrote a poem for my stepmother.

I ate my father's charred bones for supper.

M   I   N   U   T   E   S

Greek Goddesses' Marketing Committee Meeting (GGMCM)
held 15 March 2020.
Venue: Via Zoom due to COVID-19 isolation restrictions.

Present: Hera, Demeter, Styx, Artemis, Thetis, Electra, Aphrodite, Nemesis, Themis, Hestia, Athena, Tyche, Selene, Pheme, Euterpe and Hebe.

Apologies: Metis, Enyo, Keres, Doris, Merope and Eris (who advised she may also miss the next meeting due to chaos).

Chair/Throne: Artemis

Minute taker: Calliope (The Chair acknowledged Calliope's work in presenting previous minutes as an interesting mix of lyric and epic poetry, but requested a more business-like style going forward).

General business:
1.   **Remediation Working Group update** (History to Herstory – corrective action re unacceptable mythology)
       1.1.   As the result of a highly successful campaign by GGMC, formal charges have been laid against Zeus for swallowing his pregnant first wife, Metis. It is expected that Zeus' defence team will contend the action was justified because it was intended to stop Metis from delivering a child who could usurp his power, consistent with clause XXIVc of Greek law, 'The Natural Order of Things'. The defence may also contend that because his bid was unsuccessful, and the child Athena survived, charges should be dropped. Observers have stated they would not be surprised if Zeus draws on the contextual impact of his upbringing. His parents, Kronus and Rhea met at AA, lapsed extensively in his formative years, and lost their home by gambling 'heads and tails' with Hermes and Pan. The prosecutor is expected

14

to succeed in dismissing this material as irrelevant should it arise.

The trial commences in the intercalary month and will be closely monitored by GGMC for any potential precedents that can be leveraged. (Note: Athena and Aphrodite declared a conflict of interest and did not participate in discussion of this item as their father is the alleged perpetrator. As both Zeus' sister and wife, Hera also excused herself. All three members asked that their disclosures and shared view of Zeus as a brutal, domineering asshole be recorded in the minutes). The Committee approved petty cash expenditure for Nemesis to create banners for the trial, notably, 'Justice for Metis', 'The noose for Zeus' and 'Zeus—your goose is cooked'.

1.2.   In a separate case, Dionysus is lodging a claim against Zeus for removing him from his mother, Semele, before he was born. That Zeus then sewed the foetus inside his thigh until it was time for the boy to be born, is a classic example of a man usurping the role of a woman and criminal entitlement. The GGMC agreed to formally write to Dionysus (aka Bacchus) acknowledging his advocacy for the maternal role and rights of women, and to offer any assistance (with the usual disclaimer that making casseroles is now considered repressive and sexist). Noting Dionysus took over from Hestia as an Olympic god, the Committee also wished him well for Paris in 2024. As God of Wine, the Committee also indicated they would waive the usual disclosure requirements should he wish to sponsor their Christmas-in-Hekatombaion celebrations.

1.3.   Artemis indicated she had formally applied to the Office of Titles to revoke some of her portfolios. As Goddess of the virgin moon, the hunt, wild animals, fertility and childbirth, apparently young men have assumed she invented Tinder. As such, she no longer wants to assume any hunt or animal-related responsibilities. The goddess expects this to progress unopposed before the end of 2020. She is agitating for this to come into effect prior to Gamelion New Year celebrations.

1.4.   As Goddess of the Hearth, Hestia previously gave up her seat as one of the original Twelve Olympians to Dionysus to tend the sacred fire on Mt. Olympus. On reflection, she received poor industrial advice, and now sees that this is a strategy often used by the patriarchy, which is ironic given the well-documented inability of gods to multi-task. She has formally applied to resume her seat as an Olympian, and is lobbying for this to be on a job-share basis, creating an important opportunity for another goddess to advance. Hestia has also asked the alchemists to investigate the feasibility of installing a gas-log fire on Mt Olympus, as it is demeaning for a goddess to function as a human pilot light. Hestia declined Nemesis' generous offer to assist with placards at this time, but will advise should the need arise.

2.   **COVID-19 update**

2.1.   Several goddesses reported it was easier to work from home, although difficult to juggle children and home-schooling. The self-paced 'Don't take-aeons-to-learn-Greek' language app had proved a boon for younger deities.

2.2.   Aphrodite noted that as she had been publicised widely in the Venus de Milo sculpture, the complementary hand sanitiser issued to all Committee members was insensitive. The Committee issued a heartfelt verbal and written apology.

Any other business:

• As Goddess of Eternal Youth, Hebe suggested members turn on the 'Touch up my appearance' feature on Zoom for subsequent meetings. Although it was agreed a soft focus is flattering, after much discussion, the Committee voted not to take this action as it perpetuated the objectification of women.

• As Goddess of Gossip, Pheme asked Aphrodite if the rumours about her and Eros were true. Aphrodite advised the Committee, what while it is none of anyone's business, she had divorced Eros. She explained this was largely attributable to a long-running dispute; Eros removed her child, Pothos, at birth claiming Aphrodite bore a son. While acknowledging she was still under the influence of analgesia from labour, Aphrodite is adamant the baby was a daughter and has fought unsuccessfully for custody for many years. She can only see Pothos through artistic representations, noting they consistently refer to and depict Pothos as 'a man without a beard'.

• Calliope advised she no longer wished to be minute-taker and left the meeting, her use of expletives suggesting she is unlikely to return. Euterpe offered to undertake this task with a proviso that the minute format should alternate between a business style and free verse to depart from traditional male writing conventions.

Next meeting: To be advised.

The Chair/Throne thanked all members for their participation. As part of getting to know each other better, she suggested that members bring one favourite item from home and a lyre or harp to share their favourite melody at the next meeting.

Artemis also asked that participants think about ways they could adapt the Committee's traditional fundraising strategies to account for pandemic restrictions. Selene advised she had heard about a game 'My urn, your turn' where a photograph of an urn is displayed online. People pay to submit guesses about who made the piece, how long it needed to be fired and how many tetradrachm coins it holds. All agreed this sounded like a lot of fun, and Selene undertook to find out more and report back to the group.

There being no other business, the meeting concluded at 11. 05 am EET.

Grey Wolf
Dasha Maiorova

I am tired of breaking my bones for unworthy men. None were less worthy than that child, that greedy hero of whom they'll sing through the ages: Prince Ivan. Was I not all things to you? Was I not pliable enough? Strong enough? Silent enough? Could I have been faster, or more beautiful?

I carried you – physically, if not figuratively – on my back, young Prince Ivan. You with your fine, slender build and high-toned voice. They'll make a man of you in the stories. Me – they'll say I came from nowhere, offered assistance readily and fell over my feet to aid you. They'll say you thanked me, bowed three times, and I disappeared back into the forest.

A common saying in Russia: "'Thank you' is too generous, I'll take my payment in coin."

I would take mine in the safety you promised.

Imagine the field, in summer, as the sun sets over the taiga. You've never seen the sky so purple, and the belt of gold that reams over the pines, it's more precious than your coveted firebird cage. Or the gold-plaited mantle. Or the silent Princess Helen.

The hoof prints from your gold-maned horse still mark plods in the soft earth. Your two brothers took your flaxen-haired, quiet bride, and left pieces of you scattered across the grass.

Crows gather, already tasting the morsels of your sweet flesh. How pale your skin, even before your brothers hewed you, limb from limb and threw your parts across the clearing.

They laughed while they did so. I know because the crows speak of it as they tread over your cumbersome ribs and peek closer for soft liver, or a kidney, or a piece of your naïve heart.

"–wish they cracked the skull! Oh, how delicious, to taste the brain of a prince."

"Be glad for this offering. An ample feast."

"Ha! Hardly an inch of fat on him – still a boy, shame."

One, ready to prize your ripe, right eye for her chick, glosses out her dark wings. She senses my nearness in the final moment. The chick, ugly and pink, squawks. Indignant hunger. I snatch her in my jaws.

Other crows take flight in flurries of coal-black. Cursing me for claiming their spoil. My kind, when there was a kind such as mine, we wouldn't eat your leavings. We don't feast on the fallen.
We made it fall.
"Grey Wolf – I beg you, release my chick!"
I paw the ball of fluff from one paw to another. The scent of Ivan's entrails is in my nostrils. Sweet as berries. The scent of sanctuary lost.
"Hmm… I wonder. What a snack," I muse.
"Let her go, you – you foul dog-bitch!"
Pecks at my ear. She's a feisty one.
"Ey! Alright then, listen, Crow-Mother. I'll let your offspring live, but you must do something for me. Fly off and bring me two types of water: one still, from a deep well, and one which sparkles – dew from the needles of the tallest pine in the forest will do. Yes, you'll have to work in the early morning, but do not fear. I'll watch over your youngling for now."
Her watchful eye shines with panic and the concern only a mother has for a child left in the company of her most feared foe. Let her think what she will of me. The chick quivers beneath my paw. I hear it's beating heart. Poor little thing, you keep going like that and you'll burst.
"I do not trust a wolf to keep its promise," Mother-Crow intones.
"I am not a wolf."

In Ivan's story (it's always Ivan's story), he is the third brother to try and catch the thief stealing the golden apples in his father's orchard. The others, on two consecutive nights, fall asleep, and fail to report the thief to father Tsar Berendey.
The nervous little nothing of a boy, so anxious not to fall asleep, washes his face with dew. And in the lowest point of night, sees a firebird pick at the precious fruit. Why Berendey had the apple trees to begin with is never answered. He acquired it the same way other powerful warlords obtain whatever desirous thing they like.
He slew and he plundered.
But you didn't hear it from me. I was meant to be getting on the good side of the Tsars at that stage. They banished us Greys to the cruel, unkind forest, called us names like Baba Yaga and hag, and

slew those of us who came close to towns and villages. Heroes, they called themselves.

Anyway, Ivan – crafty Ivan, clever Ivan – sneaks up to the firebird, plucks a single glowing feather from its glorious tail as it flies off, and in the morning, presents it to his father.

It's the greed of men that keeps this story going, you following me, little Chick?

I warned him. I warn every single fool who might take this path. I carved the words into the pillar myself. Follow on straight down the road, and be cold and hungry. Go right, and you'll be safe but your horse will perish. Go left, and you'll perish, and so will your horse. I admit, I could have worded it differently: the path ahead is cold and bare, but follow it, and leave me be.

What does Ivan do? He gets his horse killed, of course. Thinking he'll just get another. What is it with these men who think they'll acquire something newer? Of course, all was given to him from a young age. I admit, I ate his horse. I sprang from the edge of the grass, where I'd been dozing. I love to be under the wide sky, though it is dangerous to hold a wolf's form in this day and age. I tore into the tight red muscle of the neck of his beautiful horse. It went down majestically: a glorious, forlorn death. He knew, the stallion, to submit to me. Knew submission from his stabling in a Tsar's court, knew what it was to be gelded, whipped, beaten about the head. Blinkered, so as not to see what he might be missing. His lashes veiled his wide liquid eyes as he fell. I think it is a form of love, to hunt, to catch in this thrall. His great hooves beat the air. He came to rest as I clung to his shuddering back, my teeth latched to his neck.

How delicious, the meat of a fine thoroughbred.

I would not turn my teeth to the rider, for that was not the deal. The plaque, my solemn vow and promise to all those that pass here.

I heard weeping, a sound I know too well. In the stories, they say the mighty Prince Ivan walked for a day, listening over his shoulder for the sounds of the grey wolf in pursuit of him. I'd outpace him in the blink of an eye. No, the young boy wept to see his beautiful steed torn before him. I do not shame him for this. It is not wrong for a man to weep. Especially not for the demise of his worthy companion, who carried him all those days.

He had a narrow, pale face, with large blue eyes. A spray of blood freckled his cheeks and the linen tunic he wore. The raw leather of his boots smelled new, and I caught the scent of blood in the blisters of his heels and toes. He might have been a peasant, but for the gold emblem of the stag belted over his hip. So I knew he was a son of Berendey.

His voice trembled as he pleaded with me not to take his life.

A saying in Russia: "Two deaths will not happen–"

"But one is inevitable." He concluded.

I narrowed my yellow eyes. "Boy, how could I break a promise written in stone? You knew what would become your horse if you came this way. You had a choice, but you valued your life above your beast's."

Morose, he described his quest for the firebird, his desire to please his father – his father, who he proudly admitted was Tsar Berendey himself. Who might be persuaded to offer sanctuary to one like me, I realised.

I laughed. "You could have ridden for three years and never found that firebird! But hear me, Prince Ivan, I will assist you in your quest, and I ask in return only that you promise my safety – that I might walk and live in the kingdom of your father, and not be hunted as you have hunted all of us Greys out of existence. I am one of the last, and I don't intend to spend the end of my days in a house on chicken feet like my sorceress cousin Yaga."

Imagine, he did not even ask my name. I did what I swore I would never do, because he was complacent, that boy, and had a sweet look about him: I lowered myself.

"Climb on my back, and hold tight to my fur. I'll carry you to the fortress of Tsar Afron – he keeps his precious songbird in a golden cage. It's a gaudy work of art, lad, and I warn you now: do not touch the cage, but you can swipe the bird while it preens. It's quite captivated by its reflection in a mirror."

I suppose you know what happened next.

The raven chick puffs its feathers. New quills prod from the grey-purple of its skin. The opposite of a firebird, this little fluffball. I pass my tongue over its plumage.

"There, all clean now. Your mother will return soon, little one."

Ivan stroked the cage – of course he did. The boy, just like his father, coveting shiny objects. At home, a tree that produced apples coated in gold leaf, and under his coat, a bird shimmering golden and bright as fire, and yet he wanted that cage too. As punishment, when Tsar Afron heard the sweet tinkling of the bell fixed to the top of the cage, he hauled Ivan before him and demanded for compensation a horse with a mane of gold – the one belonging to his sworn enemy, Tsar Kusman.

When Ivan failed to steal the horse, Kusman, stroking his beard, studded with the same gemstones as on the tinkling bridle on his horse, proposed Ivan remedy his latest attempted theft by taking the most valuable prize of all: the beautiful princess Helen, daughter of warrior-chief Tsar Dalmat.

"Flaxen-haired, and I hear Dalmat cut out her tongue when she was a child – otherwise she's untouched: the perfect woman!" Kusman throttled with laughter. "Bring me the girl, this virgin Helen, and you can have your horse and the bridle with the bells that betrayed you!"

When Ivan tearfully told me of his mission, I bared my teeth.

"You moron! Why did you touch the cage, and then the bridle! Does your greed know no bounds?" At the venom in my words, I calmed myself. The end-game was a greater goal, I could tolerate the child's foolishness for beautiful sanctuary.

"I did wrong," Ivan wailed. The great Ivan, Ivan the brave! Oh, Vanya, my young fool.

I seethed. I told him I would be in his service, I would find Helen myself and bring her to him.

I saw her in her garden walled by stone. She was accompanied by a troupe of guards, each wielding a shashka sabre. Helen fell back and never said a word, did not even lift her eyes to them, or to me, as I tore out their throats.

"Helen, I am no wolf. I was once a girl like you, but became more than woman. I turned Grey, lived in the forest and learned incantations and how to shape the world to my will. I could kill you,

22

as I killed your sentinels, or you could come with me and be a wife to a son of Berendey."

I must admit, I half wish she hadn't climbed astride my back. I despise a compliant woman.

I suspect the look in Ivan's eyes when he saw Helen was the same he had when he gazed upon the firebird cage and the gold-linked bridle. These forbidden treasures linked in their purpose: cage, bridle, girl. Capture.

"How can I ever think to part from her?" he asked as he replaced the veil over Helen's face. He could not bring himself to touch her, she was that precious to him already. Oh, Vanya. A look like that will get you killed.

"Have you ever witnessed a Russian wedding, dear Chick? Throughout the feasting, guests shout: 'Gorka! Gorka!' Bitter! Bitter! The bride and groom must kiss to sweeten their drinks. Wedding guests, love their drinks, and none more than those in the party of Tsar Kusman.

"His breath smelled of boar meat and cabbage when he carried his fresh, washed bride to the bedchamber. The leering shrieks of his guests followed them down the corridor – bitter!"

He'd been feasting all day, the Tsar, and pulled his small-boned wife down to the mattress. Belched these words into her ear: "Now, my love, show me what fine girls come are made in the kingdom of Dalmat…"

A rough hand searches for a small, ripe breast and finds instead a row of nipples. My face, which I made pale and perfect, moulding the cheekbones into arches, breaking down my nose with spell and mortar, softened into a smile, despite the ache. My lips I painted red with the juice of wild berries. My teeth, still canine-keen, glinted as I licked them.

"Oh, but husband, don't you care to enjoy your new bride?" I asked. He could not remove his hand, it seemed, from my chest, in spite of his discovery. Merciless, I sunk my teeth into his throat. I will not deny that the taste of a man who has eaten well, tastes best. Freedom tastes better, however. I imagined walking across the steppes of Berendey's tsardom, Ivan might even persuade him to grant me a territory of my own. I heard strong women might fare well in the Rus.

The morning of my 'wedding' to Kusman, while I broke down my legs to better resemble Helen, Ivan bowed to me, three times. He bent his back low, the lowest supplication a prince could ever make. "You have given me all I ever wanted," he said. "Thank you, Grey Wolf."

It's not done, to remind the host of the conditions of a bargain struck in such times. What's the saying? Friendship is friendship but service is service?

Leather strap between my teeth, I nodded, broke my crooked dog's shin so it might better match the ankle I designed. One to rival's Helen's small ankle. My scream sent the crows colliding from the trees. And off I went, the mock bride to Kusman's tent.

For that boy, I broke my bones. This boy they will title Hero. Gallant Prince Ivan, who rode on the back of a grey wolf to set his lover free. He clawed his fingers into the fur of my shoulders. His hips bucked as he rode me. More passion in that, than his touchless gawping at mortal Helen.

How deeply he must have slept, curled beside her in that shining glade as I was led to the wedding bed of the belching Tsar. The firebird feather burned a beacon through the forest. Was it Afron who directed the brothers to Ivan, nestling in the ferns? They crept upon the couple, the crow-chick tells me. She nestles closer between my wolf-again paws. One brother grasped Helen's veil, and twisted her hair in his fist. She could not shout, of course. Her mouth opened in an empty wail. The other plunged his sword into Vanya's chest, piercing one lung. He sank onto the boy, trampling the firebird feather into the dirt.

A dull copper still glimmers in the earth, but you cannot fix the broken filigree of feathers, Chick, your mother has likely warned you of this.

"We need not even threaten her, brother!" the other laughed. "This must be Helen, the daughter of Dalmat, and she has no tongue to tell of Vanya's fate. Her ransom is worth more than firebird to our father!"

They cut pieces from him, carved him, slender limb from slender limb, and tossed the parts across the glade. And that is how I found him.

"Ah - Crow-Mother, here you have returned! Your chick is safe and well. Have you brought the waters? One still, and one sparkling?"

First, I must gather all his parts. I will sprinkle the water upon him, a communion of sorts. I know the sacred words to say. It takes time. It takes sacrifice. Even a Prince cannot heal in a moment. My magic is not without cost.

My gums ache. Canines missing, ground into paste. What is a Grey without her teeth? I will not hunt again. I needed the paste to put the broken child back together. The rising sun scorches my eyes. I cannot look away so I bind a length of cloth from Ivan's ruined tunic over my face. I tore away my eyelids so he might see again. Berendey would not accept a faulted-son returned to him, and I would not achieve my sanctuary.

I hear a yawn.

"I slept so deeply," Ivan says. Ferns rustle as he stretches out. A hero, woken from his slumber, to prevail this day. A hero revived by a Grey woman, of whom they will say nothing, but that I returned, grateful to be of service, to the forest.

An old saying: Seryy vsyo svezyot.

The Grey will bear it all.

Kids
Maeve Henry

'Keep safe while I'm gone,' I told them. 'Check the paws,
see if they're white. And use your ears. His voice isn't kind.
Remember how he used to snap, remember his rages.
 If he comes, don't let him in -'

but they were kids.
They wanted to think his matted fur was white.
They wanted his voice to be chalk soft. They couldn't help it,
they opened the door.
And, no, I didn't save them.
The story told it wrong. I cut him open
but they were gone. His heart was empty.
I didn't sew him up with stones instead. There was no well.
I am the one who carries them inside me, calcified.

A Thousand Ships
Nicky Zhang

Aphrodite comes to me in the middle of the night. With a wave of her hand she freezes time. Beside me, Menelaus' snore is cut off mid-thunder, and the candle flames lay suspended in the air like gold coins beaten into strange shapes.

People say I'm the most beautiful woman in the world, but the Goddess' beauty radiates out of her like moonlight on a clear night, bleaching all else into insignificance. She gestures at me to make the proper obeisances, which I do, stumbling out of bed to cower at her feet. Her toenails are painted red with a glittering diamond sheen. I can't take my eyes off them.

'Gel acrylics,' she says, noticing. And then she laughs. 'Never mind. That's thousands of years in your future. Forget I said anything.'

I surreptitiously look up. She is eating an apple. Its skin shines golden, but even from here I can see that the flesh is bruised and brown. Still she eats it studiously, looking determined to enjoy it. A bead of juice runs down her alabaster chin.

'A guest is coming to Sparta,' she says. 'You will fall in love with him.'

Two questions come to mind but I dare not ask the first, which is why. 'Who?' I ask instead.

'A Prince of Troy. You'll like him well enough. He's pretty. I taught him how to dress.'

She looks like she expects me to thank her, so I do. And then I ask, 'What of my husband?'

She glances toward Menelaus on the bed, the tangle of chest hair, the roll of fat about his waist. 'Why do I care?' She says with a curl of the lip, takes another bite of apple, and immediately spits it out with an exclamation of disgust. She throws what's left of the apple to the ground, and it explodes into fragments next to my face.

'Anyways, just a courtesy call. Paris lands in three days. Ta.'

With that she's gone. The flames waver back to life. Menelaus' snore strikes up again.

I stay kneeling, looking at what remains of the apple. The core is rotted through with grey mould covering the seedless cavity. A half-chewed white maggot lies gleaming in the decayed flesh, still wriggling.

Hecuba and Andromache, all the Trojan women, look at me as though they know exactly why I'm here.

I cannot lie, the riches in King Priam's palace are astounding. As Queen of Sparta I wore fine wool and torques of wrought silver; in the palaces of Troy I am given robes of silk and brocade, and jewels cut with a thousand facets, set in delicate gold filigree. But they are not why I'm here.

Paris can play the lyre and sing in a sweet tenor voice, and he always smells like precious rose otto. I love running my hand over the groove where the top of his thighs meets his hips, the tantalising hollow edged by taut muscle. He is young and beautiful and very convincing, and I didn't need much convincing because it's a done deal; Aphrodite told me as much. Sometimes I wonder whether it would have still been a done deal if she hadn't shown up, but what's the point of second-guessing the Gods?

My footsteps echo in the stone hallway. I don't see her until it's too late. I walk straight into Cassandra, who recoils and then falls to her hands and knees, hissing and spitting.

The women say to ignore the Princess, but it's hard advice to follow when she is crouched on all fours bristling like a wildcat. Her head is an unsightly mess of bare scalp and half-healed welts because she tears out her hair in chunks. The women whisper that Apollo had made her insane, because she had rejected his advances. How glorious it would be to live an entire life unnoticed by the Gods.

I mutter an apology and try to step past, but she flings out her arms to stop me. 'Your niece is dead because of you.'

I have three nieces. I saw them all last year at the Mysteries of Samothrace. They share the same flat nose of King Agamemnon but the clever dark eyes of my sister Clytemnestra. 'They live and prosper in Mycenae,' I say.

She shakes her head. 'Iphigenia's body lies at Aulis, her throat cut. Because of what you did.'

Andromache must have put her up to it. She hated me the moment I showed up. 'Everyone says you're a liar, and mad,' I say as I push past, knocking Cassandra's arm aside.

Behind me she emits a long thin laugh which abruptly stops, like a kithara with its strings cut.

Five days later the black sails appear over the horizon. The Achaeans had mustered a fleet at Aulis, waiting for a wind that Artemis held back. To please the Goddess, Agamemnon had offered his own daughter as sacrifice.

The Achaeans take up residence. Along a mile of coast there are beached ships and tents and hundreds of cookfires. At night their distant camp glows like a swarm of fireflies.

The Trojan army clears the nearby villages, bringing people and livestock inside the walls. A thick animal stench hangs over the streets, and every time I go into the city there are people jeering and pointing. Someone throws a rotten apple and it smashes into the headrest of my litter, missing my face by an inch. The smell reminds me of that night in my bedchamber, Aphrodite's exclamation of disgust.

All this because of me. Panic is a gaping hole at the bottom of my stomach. When I go about my day there are moments when I would forget, but the churn always comes back, and every time it comes back it feels like a fish bone stuck at the base of my throat. I fight the constant urge to bend over double, to curl into a ball on the ground. Already Paris tires of my black moods, the fact that he can't curb my weeping by simply offering his body, his sweet words, or else gold and jewels. Several times I have caught him making eyes at the chambermaids.

Meanwhile the Achaeans rush the city gates, are pushed back, and the Trojans swarm out in pursuit, all the way to the rough barricades of the Achaean camp, and are pushed back in turn. The tides of battle turn as predictably as the tides of the sea. The dead litter the plain outside the city walls. Funeral pyres are lit most nights and the lamentations of women rend the stifling air. More than once I hear them mention me by name. The Whore of Sparta, they call me. Go back where you came from. Go before you kill all our husbands, fathers and sons.

Priam and Prince Hector order the guards to search out those women and flog them for besmirching the royal name. I am grateful, even though I do not deserve it.

Soon there comes a day when the fighting ceases and a woman comes to fetch me. 'Paris and Menelaus have agreed to fight for you in single combat,' she says, her voice husky with relief. 'You will go with the victor, and both armies will cease warring after.'

My heart lifts and then sinks. 'A fight to the death?' 'Yes. I expect it's to your liking.'

She rushes away before I can comprehend her meaning. A sob rises. I swallow it down and it sits like a stone in my chest.

Priam sends a messenger to call me to the ramparts. When I arrive, he gestures to the armies standing ready outside the city walls, and asks me to name the Achaean heroes. I point out Agamemnon the King of Kings, wily Odysseus, huge Ajax with his two-handed blade, old Nestor and his many warrior sons.

'I have sons too,' says Priam, narrowing his eyes against the sun. 'And strong walls. Let them come.'

Paris advances past the Trojan line and into the field of single combat. Menelaus comes to greet him, wearing his battered cuirass and carrying his sword with the sweat-darkened hilt.

Paris' armour has shining clasps of silver and a fine gold inlay. He starts at the sight of Menelaus, takes two steps back as though considering fleeing, but Hector thrusts him forward again with a sharp admonition.

A calm settles over me as I watch the fight commence, my two husbands taking turns poking at each other with their spears. I am familiar with both their bodies, the old and the new. The outcome is not in doubt. I can already feel myself spirited onto the Achaean ships and borne back to Sparta on a fair wind.

The Trojans gasp in terror as Menelaus seizes a gap and throws Paris onto his back, grabs him by the helmet and drags him backwards. Paris scrabbles and skids to find purchase, his fingers clawing deep grooves into the red dirt. Menelaus casts aside his spear and draws his sword; the next moment he has only an empty helmet in his hand. The hot sun beats down on the field and hundreds of pairs of eyes search the empty space where Paris should be.

The Achaeans scream in frustration and rattle their spears against their shields. The crowd atop the ramparts chatter like frightened birds. 'The Gods were prohibited to intervene,' I hear the seer Helenus shout above the uproar. 'Someone broke the rules.'

I feel a tug on my robe. I look, and an old woman is pulling me away from the din. 'Paris has been transported to your bedchamber. He lies waiting for you there, beautiful and unhurried as though he had never seen battle.'

I gape at her for a long moment. No one has ever accused me of being quick on the uptake.

Shining from the old eyes is a gaze as luminous as the stars. I blink, and the flimsy glamour slips. As Aphrodite pulls me into an unattended hallway already the charm is melting from her like old wax. Here is her swan-like neck, here is her milky bosom. She is still tugging on my sleeve with her red-painted nails but I draw to a stop. Anger bursts in me like the Scamander overrunning its banks.

'It's over,' I say. 'Menelaus won. I will return to him.' She laughs at me. 'You belong to Paris.'

'I belong to no one,' I snap. 'I'm not some thing to be traded away for an apple. Yes, I know about the contest, I know what you offered him. I should have refused you from the start. You say you can see the future. Did you forsee all this?'

'I am a *God*,' she says, drawing herself up to her full height, all eight feet of her, the top of her golden head bristling toward the ceiling. 'I know the past and future, the paths of all mortal men.'

'You knew what would happen and you did it anyway.' I think about the corpses on the plain baking under the sun. 'I wasn't yours to give. You should have sold yourself if you wanted it so much. You would have fetched a better price.'

She strikes me across the face then, and I fall to the floor as pain explodes red across my eyes.

'Do not provoke me,' she says, and her voice echoes rasping down the stone corridor. 'Do as you're told, or I will make this war last forever. I'll make the Trojans and Achaeans fight until every last one is dead, and they will all die cursing your name.'

With a crack she blinks out of existence, leaving the smell of singed air behind her.

The war doesn't last ten years. It lasts barely six months. Never believe a word the bards sing.

The news of Hector's death reaches me while I'm in my rooms, weaving a tapestry of our heroes. My hands go numb and I drop my distaff. 'But Achilles isn't fighting,' I stammer.

The woman wipes her eyes with the corner of her cloak. 'He swore revenge after the Prince killed his friend. He was in such a rage, ma'am. After he killed the Prince he... he...'

I have to shake her by the shoulders to get her to tell me, and when I hear it, it is a trickle of ice water down my spine. Hector's body, dragged behind Achilles' chariot, mutilated.

Desecrated. Gone to the dogs.

I try to stand, and instead I stumble and fall to my knees. I press both palms to the cold ground and retch. Hector, the last and greatest of Troy's defenders. He and Priam were the only ones in this city who had always been kind to me.

I do not follow the women as they flock to comfort Andromache, she would never allow me to bear witness to her grief. I keep to my rooms, taking my meals there, weaving my tapestry, waiting for my accusers to beat down the door.

No one comes. The palace has forgotten about me because Achilles refuses to return Hector's body for his rites, preferring to condemn his soul for eternity. It takes many days, and divine intervention, but finally Priam is conveyed to the Achaean camp to make his case. I never learned what was said that night between grief-torn Priam and equally grief-torn Achilles, but the next morning Hector's body was brought to the gates on a cart, covered with a blood-stained sheet.

The pyre is lit. The lamentations are spoken. And I stand there watching Priam through the smoke, his body like a gnarled fir, his eyes dim with grief.

Paris stands beside me, his jaw set. I don't know what he's thinking, and I don't care.

After the rites I follow Priam as he staggers away on his walking stick. 'Father,' I choke out. 'It's my fault and I'll answer for it, whatever you name. Send me back to Menelaus. Send me back in pieces. Throw me from the walls. I'm ready to pay the price.'

He turns. His old man's skin hangs loose from his skull. There is death in his eyes. 'It's not your fault,' he says.

I could have accepted any insult but this. How does one begin to refute such a monstrous lie?

'The house of Atreus has been after Troy's riches for generations,' the old man says, and I now see that he is still trying to be kind. 'Agamemnon only needed a reason.'

'But I gave him that reason.'

'He would have found one regardless.' Priam inclines his head at me, turns and keeps walking. His voice travels back faintly. 'War is a man's game. It wasn't ever about you. How could it? You're only a woman.'

I stand on my balcony looking down at the burning city. It is an overcast night; the sky's cloudy underbelly glows red from the reflected flames. It must be what Tartarus looks like.

Ten thousand inhabitants within these ancient walls, hunted down like game. Screams splitting the air, the acrid smoke from burning thatch, this unbearable heat.

It smells like a festival. Burning human bodies are only, after all, roasted meat.

Earlier in the day I had looked up at the enormous wooden contraption, and I had wondered. But Cassandra had already shouted the warning and no one listened to that either. I sang an old Spartan lullaby and left them to their own devices. While the people ate and drank to celebrate the Achaeans' sudden departure, I sat in the darkness, waiting. Did I know what was coming? Perhaps.

A crack and she's back. Aphrodite. She teeters across the room in golden sandals with spindly heels, every step preceded by the scent of rose and jasmine.

'Come,' she says, reaching out her white hand. 'I'll save you.' I remain seated. 'No, thank you.'

She tuts. 'Don't be dramatic. My son Aeneas is taking a ship into the west. He'll found a great dynasty that would stand for a thousand years. You'll go with him and rule by his side.'

'No,' I say.

She taps her feet. 'I can transport you to his ship right now. You don't have a say in this.' 'If you do it, I'll jump into the sea.'

'I'll stop you from drowning. I'll turn you into a porpoise. What's wrong with you? People pray their whole lives for favour from the Gods.'

'And they always live to regret it. I defy you, Aphrodite.'

Her nostrils flare. 'Do you have any idea what it means to incur my wrath?' 'Do you think I care?'

She glares at me. I look back serenely.

'I finally figured it out,' I say. 'Yes, you are a God. You can punish me forever in cruel and unusual ways. You can bend my body in all the ways you desire, but you can't rule my mind.'

She laughs. 'Have you met Cassandra? Apollo cut her mind to ribbons.'

'My soul, then. Whatever it's called. There's a part of me you can't reach and you know it. I daresay it's a lot less fun when people figure this out.'

She tilts her head at me like a curious bird. 'But there's nothing left for you here.' She's right at that. Come morning this will be a city of ash.

'It's my choice,' I say.

She rolls her eyes skyward. 'Whatever. Stay then. Let the Achaeans tear you to pieces.'

She disappears. Perhaps I will see her again in this life, but I feel certain in the knowledge that I won't.

I sit alone for a while longer, watching the scenes of carnage below. I wait until the fighting comes closer, until the ringing of swords and the shouting of men are directly beneath my feet. Someone bellows like a sacrificial bull. 'Where is the bitch that launched a thousand ships?'

I stand, arrange my mantle, and go down to meet my fate.

Maiden of the Southern Forest
Anthea Yang

Tucked into the breast
of the rooster
in the breath
between autumn and spring
the earth exhales a gentle
breeze
      lands at the tip
of a sword
      falls on the damp
soil of the forest floor.

The sword is
      an extension
of the mind.
The sword is
      the opening
and closing of two
swinging doors
      touching only by
the air that it moves.

The sword is
the maiden
calm in the face of combat
harmonious in movement
      —to expand the body
is to carve the space
it needs to move through
      —to be the sharpened tip
and the current that guides it.

陰   On this side of the hill
now there are clouds
— in the breath

between autumn and spring
chaos dances the most
beautiful dance with light—
陽　　On that side of the hill
now the sun is shining.

The Tenant of Rookwood Hall
Louise Pieper

I had gone out into the world and entered upon a new life. I found it much to my liking. With a home of my own I could do as I pleased. Such unseemly independence in a woman so young could not help but cause speculation and suspicion in a rural village in the ninth year of Queen Victoria's reign, but I endured this as the price of my freedom. I had lived what felt like a hundred years at the beck and call of others who placed no value on my desires. I would not do so again merely to allay the fears or gratify the curiosity of my neighbours.

Early one morning, late in October, I avoided the village gossips by setting out from my back door. I locked it behind me and dropped the key into the pocket of my walking dress, then strode through the bare orchard and crossed the stile to the pastures. The path hugged the base of Gerth's Ribs, a basalt cliff named for the giantess said to have defended the Fell in ancient times.

The Fell rose up and the clouds pressed down and perhaps I should have felt stifled by their smothering frowns. Perhaps I should have feared the dreaded Gytrash or the fairies of the Rath. But I had planned a brisk walk to the nearest town where I would collect a new book and I was answerable to no-one for how I spent my time. With that luxury my spirit soared, carried aloft on the wings of the cold breeze.

From the peak of the Fell, within two miles of Bishops Beck, the road lay before me like a hedge-trimmed brown ribbon. But as I descended on the narrow sheep's path, something kept pace with me in the shadow of the hedgerow. Its eyes flashed gold and I caught the silhouette of a great bristled lion's mane around its head.

Was it the Gytrash?

Fear crashed onto me and my blood leapt, as if my heart tried to push its way out of my chest. I smothered my cry and broke into a run, not wanting the creature to block my passage to the road. My boots crushed the frost which lingered still on the thin grass. I heard a pounding approach and flung myself at the stile. As I came pell-mell through the gap in the hedge, a horse appeared on the road. It reared in fright, slipped on a patch of ice and fell, tossing down its rider.

I threw myself off the stile and rushed to help, fearing the man knocked senseless or trampled. He cursed and rolled over as I reached him.

"I am sorry," I cried. "Are you hurt?"

He scowled, darkening a visage that was already grim.

"Of course, I am hurt," he said, as if he could not believe I would ask such a stupid question.

I put out my hand and he hesitated a moment then clasped it and let me help him to his feet. It was as well, for his left leg seemed scarcely able to support him.

"So, you are not some fairy sprite," he said gruffly as I took some of his weight on my shoulders. "I feared you had bewitched poor Sirrah."

He gestured to his horse which had scrambled upright and stood trembling just out of reach.

"I must get to town," he said. "I need a nurse."

"A doctor for your leg?" I asked, confused.

"No, a nurse for a babe that needs care. I cannot–"

He reached for the rein and would have toppled if I had not caught him.

"I go to Bishops Beck," I said. "I could take a message. You should not ride far in your state."

I looked around as if I might spy his house somewhere nearby. There was only the road and the hedges and the Fell looming above us.

"Rookwood Hall is but half a mile," he said, glaring at the ice in the road. "As well I did not bring the child with that fall..."

I felt not exactly guilty, but involved in his misfortune, and I said, "I will help you if I can Mr...?"

"Every," he said promptly. "Every of Rookwood Hall. You are very good, Miss...?"

"Grey. Jane Grey."

"If you would return to the Hall with me, Miss Grey, and mind the baby, I can have my man see to my leg and send another to town with a message for a nurse."

I agreed, but I had always lacked common sense when taken by surprise.

Rookwood Hall was a gloomy house, shadowed by the Fell and the dark woods which bracketed it. I shivered as we entered the flagged courtyard and three elderly men emerged from the stable.

"Ellis, see to Sirrah," Mr Every commanded. "Acton, to me. Currer, show Miss Grey up to the nursery."

They hurried to their tasks. The one who led me inside scampered ahead, giving me no chance to dawdle. The house was warm and well-appointed, but it seemed empty. He opened the door to a snug room at the end of the upper hallway. The glow from a fire illuminated a bed, washstand, chair and table, and a cradle in the corner. Within lay a tiny sleeping baby and I realised Mr Every had not said whether the infant was a boy or a girl. I turned back to the servant and found him already out the door.

"What is the baby's name?" I called after him.

"Er, eh…ahn," he muttered and fled.

"Ann?" I asked the silence. "John? Jane?"

Well, it was strange, but it would only be for one night.

I tended to the baby's needs and my own and when I woke, I felt cold and stiff although the fire still burned merrily in the grate and my bed looked as soft as swansdown. Again, I fed her a cup of warm milky gruel, changed her cloths, swaddled her, and sang her lullabies. I could not see why Mr Every had been so anxious for her. She was sweet and happy with no fever or mark of illness.

I turned from the cradle to find a fresh tray on the table, but no sign of the servant who had brought it. I ate my breakfast and then I fed and changed and rocked the child and told her stories of Jack Robin and Jenny Wren until we both fell asleep. When I woke I fed the babe and called her sweet Jenny Wren and changed her cloths and when I woke I fed the babe and rocked her and felt a great weariness and when I woke I fed Jenny and she smiled at me as I played the game of counting her toes. I wondered if Mr Every had found a nurse in the town and I fed Jenny and glanced out of the window and thought I glimpsed him riding into the spring-budding wood with a large black dog running at his horse's heels.

I fed Jenny and changed her and when I woke, I fed her and should have liked to brush her hair, it was growing so long. The warm breeze through the window brought the scent of meadowsweet and when I woke, I fed Jenny and played clapping games with her. I felt stiff and weary, but Jenny made me smile, calling me Mama as little ones do when it is the only word they know. When I woke I wondered if the nurse would arrive early enough for me to still make my way to Bishops Beck and walk home and I fed Jenny and sang her songs and we listened to the cries of the rooks as they gathered to roost.

When I woke I fed my sweet Jenny and she frowned at me and chewed on the spoon and I felt past her new front teeth to where her gums had swollen and called her a poor little lamb and showed her from the window that the trees of the wood were gowned in red and gold. I woke in the night with Jenny wailing and I dipped the corner of a cloth in cold water for her to chew on.

As I picked her up, a voice from the doorway said, "What is that noise?"

Mr Every strode into the room, frowning thunder and casting great shadows onto the walls as he paced before the sullen fire.

"Oh, she is only teething," I said. "Is that why you were..."

Worried? Injured? Sending for a nurse?

I held Jenny on one hip and rubbed my forehead, trying to remember.

"Make it stop," he said, frowning as Jenny grizzled at the cloth.

"She needs something harder to cut her teeth on," I replied, and he took off a ring and thrust it at me. I slipped it onto my finger, thinking it would be too large and I would have to tie it on a ribbon for her, but the thick band fitted perfectly and I curled my hand so Jenny might chew on it.

"What more do you need for silence?" he said.

"Well, the nurse will be here tomorrow," I answered, "but a rattle to distract the child and a comb for her hair would be welcome."

He turned aside and I looked down at myself and wondered why I wore my walking dress in the middle of the night. Had I not...? Mr Every turned back, holding out a handsome wooden rattle and a bone comb, but when I reached to take them from him Jenny flapped the damp cloth and set up a wail and he demanded again, "Make it stop!"

I thrust the comb and the rattle into my pocket and my fingertips brushed against the old iron key which I had used to lock the back door of my cottage that morning...

The whole room seemed to tilt and darken. It was not a room at all, but a cold cave with a dirt hole instead of a window and an open fire against one smoke-blackened wall. My bed was a wretched pile of sacks on which lay a thin blanket. Jenny's cot was a nest of tangled twigs and Mr Every…

I tightened my grip on the child and she gave a sharp cry.

"Silence!" Mr Every demanded, his teeth crowding in his too-wide mouth, his eyes blazing like foxfire, his horns…

I wrenched my hand from my pocket and clenched it to stop it trembling and to let Jenny bite on the ring. We stood again in a warm nursery, with a thick blue rug and striped curtains. Mr Every was only a tall and rather forbidding man, not an inhuman monster.

He frowned at me and said, "What is wrong, Miss Grey? Why–"

A crash echoed up from somewhere deep in the house and he cursed. "Not a sound!" he ordered and left, closing the door behind him.

I sank onto my bed and sat Jenny beside me, letting her gnaw on the ring while I drew the rattle, comb, and key from my pocket. When I gripped the key, all was changed. We crouched in a cave and Jenny did not wear her fine lawn nightdress but a filthy rag of grey cloth. My own dress was worn and dirty, ragged at the hem. The rattle was nothing more than a pinecone and the comb an old curved bone. I shoved them back into my pocket and tucked the key inside my bodice where it pressed cold against my skin clearing my head for the first time in…

I knew not how long I had been in that room. Jenny had been a swaddled infant when I arrived not a child speaking her first words. Mr Every had plucked me from the roadside because I was of use to him, with no more thought to my wishes than I would give in taking up a walking stick. I pressed my lips together holding in a cry of anger. He had said we must be silent.

Why?

I drew Jenny close and crept out of the cave. How different everything looked – no comfortable hall, no elegant furnishings, and shining lamps. Instead, a rough patch of ground led to a mound of stones, over which I peered into a cavern. Mr Every sat at one end on a stone chair flanked by flickering braziers. All his household stood before him, even his horse and his great black dog, which was no dog but the Gytrash. As he was no mere Mr Every. Tall and bone-thin, mantled in a cloak of dark feathers with his dark brow horned, who could he be but King Avallen of the Rath, the fairy king of the Fell?

He railed at the servants for their noise, fearing it would draw the notice of poachers in the wood or late travellers on the road. They grovelled before him, hunched and spiked as hedgehogs, sweeping the floor behind them with their furry squirrel tails.

"I want no human seeking us," he said. "Three nights and the child has been ours a twelvemonth and will be lost to the world. A mist will distract them, as will these..." He threw a handful of white pebbles to the ground, crying out the local word for thirteen – "Edderadix!" – and where each pebble fell there leapt up a full-grown, milk-white ewe. The strange servants fluttered their dragonfly wings as they herded the sheep from the cavern.

Perhaps I gasped my surprise. The head of the monstrous Gytrash lifted from its paws and turned to gaze at the pile of stones behind which I crouched. I darted back into the cave, made a sling for Jenny with the blanket, and crawled through the hole. Out on the Fell, I glanced at the near-full moon and then I ran.

I would have run for the road and for Bishops Beck, but a thick mist rose from below and I prayed it would not overtake me. I almost wept with relief to recognise a pile of moon-silvered stones and to put my feet on the path back to my cottage. And then Jenny cried out in pain with her tooth, or in indignation at this jostling frantic dashing through the night, and from behind us came the pounding sounds of pursuit.

Closer and closer came the panting of the Gytrash. Closer came the heavy thumping of its great paws and the dark horse's hooves. My breath sobbed in my throat, knowing I could not outrun them. I had no weapon, nothing I might use to protect us. I clasped Jenny and felt the damp press of the cloth I had given her.

In desperation I tugged it from between us and flung it down, crying out, "Edderadix!"

Mr Every's gold ring sparked and the cloth grew wider and wetter, spreading to become a swift-flowing stream. I ran on, knowing the fairy creatures would have to find a way around it, for they cannot cross running water.

I ran and ran, stumbling and gasping for breath. All too soon I heard again the Gytrash's bellows-breath and the clattering hooves. I clutched at a pain in my side and felt the edge of the pocket in my walking dress. Tugging out the pinecone I threw it over my shoulder.

"Edderadix!" I cried.

The ring sparked again, and a rush of cold air buffeted me. I glanced back to see a deep pine wood where only the open Fell had been. I ran on, knowing the trees would slow them.

The mist caught us as we descended and all too soon the path behind rattled with the tread of the Gytrash and the dark horse. I could not let them take Jenny. I would not let the king of the Fells use me again. Closer and closer they came and, as I reached the base of the cliff, I took the flat bone from my pocket and threw it over my shoulder.

"Edderadix," I cried, feeling the spark, and hoping it might slow the Gytrash to have some other prey.

A booming laugh shook the ground and I glanced back to see an immensely tall woman – the giantess – in a dark kirtle and a breastplate so large it would have taken two cow hides to fashion it.

"Bless you, little sister," Gerth shouted, raising her sword. "I did not think to have another chance at defeating this fiend."

She closed with the Gytrash and I ran.

There was the orchard, there the gate. I sped across the garden, drawing out the key, clasping a sobbing Jenny to my chest.

"Hush," I told her, unlocking the door. "Hush, love, we are safe home now."

"Not quite, Miss Grey," said Mr Every.

He stood on the garden path, the tall and terrible King of the Fells, his anger crackling around him like a February storm.

I stepped back, into my cottage.

"We are safe," I said. "Safe behind oak and iron. You cannot enter here."

"You must come out sometime," he said, cold as sleet, "and when you do, I will be waiting."

I hugged Jenny with one arm and raised my other hand in a fist.

"You have no dominion over us," I said. "You gave me this ring to buy our silence. Tell me, Mr Every, what Hell would it raise were I to cast it down with your magic word?"

Pale in the moonlight, he paled more. Then he nodded and stepped back, into the mist, and I closed and bolted the door.

Lucidity
Beth Spencer

Artemis sits with my mother in a clearing in the forest.
There is a fire burning, and as midwife she places
leaves one by one in a pot. I knock to get out.

The huntress touches fingertips to my brow.
So sad, my mother. Drawn and wilted.
I am the one who did this (does this).

Later, I track her round the kitchen. An endless
stream of stories. She begs me be quiet.
(I become quiet.)

Weaving black wool. (Shhh. Don't say
a word.) Reach into the soup.
Gather quiver and knife.

Wash Day at Le Carmel, Lisieux, circa 1895
Rita Tognini

There you are Thérèse Martin (now Sister Thérèse of the Child Jesus), in the cloister wash house with your sixteen Carmelite soeurs, your sisters in Christ, lined up around the stone lavatoio, each soeur's image wavering in the glassy water, their half-washed linen (wimple, tunic, vest, underskirt, menstrual rags) splayed on the stone slab; each soeur pausing from the soap and scrub, from washing away the stains— yours, ours, the world's—

You're second from left, Thérèse, between white-veiled postulants, hands on a wooden washboard, sleeves folded back. Your apron's smudged bib is pinned below the shoulders, a brown veil and white toque frames your face, hairline dark at temples. There's a wet cloth between left thumb and forefinger and a wooden paddle in right hand; ready to strike away temptations, beat out the stains— yours, ours, the world's—

You're next to your blood sister, Céline, whose camera is out front to capture your toil. She is laughing and almost clambering on to the lavatoio's rim, right hand thrust out to grab the garment dangling above the water on a pole. An older soeur leans on your shoulder, but Céline is next to you. Her laughter wimples through you, soothing the aches of solitude, penance and prayer— yours, ours, the world's—

It's definitely the flesh and blood you, Thérèse, not the Little Flower of church statues and holy pictures, milky with sanctity. It's the frank-faced-child-in-lace-trimmed-dress-and-sturdy-boots you. It's the fourteen year old, hair-atop-head-in-a-bun-to-look-older-for-the-Bishop-so-he'll-let-you-take-the-veil you. It's the clutching-the-leg-of-the-Pope-begging-him-to-let-you-enter-the-convent you. It's the grown-woman you, doing your washing, rubbing away sins— yours, ours, the world's—

It's you, Thérèse at Le Carmel with your blood sisters Pauline, Marie and Céline; and with your sisters in Christ— all menstruating in synchrony.
Thérèse, you are home.

First published in Eureka Street, Vol 30, No 2, 28/01/2020

Mokosh
Marija Poljak

The old woman extinguished the flame from her make-shift pier. She cradled the scissors and placed them by the ball of wool, alongside the basil leaves. She lay down on her pallet and took her final breaths, uttering a closing prayer and a name that had not been heard for so very long.

Mokosh.

Any God will tell you that we are only as real as humans believe us to be; only as powerful as their faith in us. So long as there is Man, there will exist God in all his forms and varieties. And so long as there is Man, the Goddess will continue to be erased and derided. And I would have wilted away were it not for the last few utterances of my name from the mouths of old crones, still clinging to the ancient ways and remembering, perhaps only in the depths of their delusion, that I was once theirs. The Goddess of women, for women. I sensed that I was ready to be forgotten, ready to disappear from the lives of women, just as I had disappeared from the lives of men so long ago.

Until I was summoned.

Mokosh.

When had I last been needed? Few had spoken my name in all these years, and even fewer had called for me specifically.

The child. Take her, Mokosh. She will need you. She will need you, because she is a she. Come and take her and spare her this life.

My dear woman, left to die alone. I know how it feels to be forgotten. But you have revived me.

This One came into the world not wanting to be born. When Nevena made her first and final entry into this Earth, the cold hit her hard. It would remain in her forever, settled deep within her bones and resurfacing whenever she had a sense of a secret.

The labour dragged on for hours, punishing her mother, and Nevena would have spent the rest of her life paying for it, were it not for me. She was safer in her mother's womb than outside of it. Those nine

47

months were the most peaceful time that mother and daughter ever had together.

When she left the birthing rooms a day and a half old, an infamous windstorm was brewing through the corridors of the black mountains. In the short time it took for father to ride to the birthing rooms, load up mother and baby, and drive back home, the branch of an intrusive elm had smashed its way through the window of the second bedroom, littering the bassinet with large shards of glass. An argument ensued between father and mother as to who was responsible until finally father had the sense to clean up the mess and mother haphazardly attached a curtain over the hole in the window. It could have been an omen. Or just a freak accident. Either way, baby slept in a cold and breezy room that night and by the next day she had already learned not to ask for very much at all.

I began to spin, to weave, to thread the child's destiny through my fingers as quickly and delicately as I could. This one required concentration. She was set on a different path, and I had to work hard to undo what had come before me.

Nevena was patient with me, and as time went on, my protection over her grew. First, I watched from afar the unwanted child; unwanted in conception, unwanted in life, and saved only by the consideration of her dying baba, and with each thread I weaved I came closer to the girl. Destiny is fickle; even I know that. There is no rushing it, and not even I can dictate it. But one can work with destiny to bend it, just enough perhaps, to set a course that is new yet subtle enough so as not to disturb the cosmic projections already in place.

I treaded carefully. I paused and considered. I amazed myself that I still had what it took to do my work. I averted many crises and saved the girl on more than one occasion, to no one's knowledge but my own.

Years went by. I never let her out of my sight. I had come to see her as mine, my special *devojka*, and all this time, she knew nothing of me. But I didn't care.

48

Nevena grew into a clever and handsome young girl, but her life had been one of great difficulty. She did not know love; had never felt it. My minor interventions were enough only to keep her safe from her wicked parents, but I could not reach deep into Nevena's heart and fill it with the warmth that ought to be imparted by a mother's touch. Towards her, they only ever showed resentment. When her mother and father realised they could produce no more children after Nevena, they saw her not as a blessing, but as a curse. She had cursed her mother's womb and poisoned their lives. But all she was ever guilty of was being born; of being born a girl, of all things. No matter. I had plans for her.

I appeared one day in the form of a middle-aged woman. Knocking on their front door, I claimed to be in search of a young apprentice. I needed someone smart but compliant, and capable of taking instructions. To seem plausible, I had already approached several homes in the village and made the same request, knowing too well that I would not find what I was looking for. Good. I knew where to find her.

My appearance was attractive; just enough to hold the husband's attention for as long as was required, but no so much as to intimidate him. My age suggested knowledgeability and experience, enough to be taken seriously, but beyond any real interest to men; certainly, no threat to the wife. But my real secret was what I had to offer: money. A meagre amount – an apprentice's wage – but money that would go directly into the hands of the parents, until the apprentice had fully completed her training.

'We have a daughter who is of little use to us. I doubt she would be of any use to you. But if you are offering to take her off our hands, and to pay us, no less, then we'd be idiots to refuse.' The father spoke directly and impetuously, as though he were doing me a favour, and not I him.

'Show me.' I said.

Nevena appeared from the washroom, having no doubt heard everything. Her almond eyes suggested a mixture of fear and curiosity. Perhaps even hope. Her fingers were tightly wound around a stale cloth, pale and wrinkled from hours spent scrubbing and washing. She stood motionless and mute, yet surprisingly stoic. 'She will do.' I said.

'Go get your things. You've got yourself a job. Consider it a miracle.'
Her father spoke to her without so much as glancing at her. Nevena
did so accordingly, if not confusedly. But she showed no sign of
resistance and uttered not a word of protest.
I waited patiently by the door whilst explaining to the father how to
collect the monthly allowance. He didn't appear to require any more
details beyond the financial ones. The mother was silent the entire
time and appeared generally satisfied. But there was a part of her
expression even I could not place.
Some mothers fail at their job, but they are still mothers.
When Nevena arrived, ready to go with me, she stood by the door
and looked at her parents. There was no emotional exchange, no
stream of love after all these years, but finally her mother did speak.
I almost thought she wouldn't even think to ask.
'And why do you need an apprentice? What is she training to
become, anyway?' 'Well,' I said. 'A midwife, of course.'
Nevena's eyelashes did a little dance, a flutter of excitement too
hidden to be noticed.
Then she followed me out of her house and towards her first home.

We travelled and rarely settled. My caravan was snug but practical
and adorned with the things we both loved. Nevena had a way with
plants and flowers and they embellished our moving home during
all seasons. I had been wrong about her; she did know love, and she
gave it in spades. It was the one thing I did not have to teach her.
The first birth she witnessed made her collapse on the ground. In all
fairness, it was a breech. Difficult for her and considerably more
difficult for the mother. But it was a happy outcome in the end. The
second time, Nevena at least remained conscious and focused on all
my instructions. By the third time, I already had her assisting me.
Her appetite to learn was simply insatiable. After a year, she was
magic. But maybe I had something to do with that. I couldn't help
myself.
Years passed, and she had long since completed her apprenticeship.
Families called for her from all towns and regions. But never her
own family. The monthly allowance was always collected
nonetheless, right up until Nevena became a midwife in her own

right. After that, only silence followed. Nevena never asked for them. Nor did she ask about me. Who was I? Why had I chosen her? How did I know… everything that I knew? Her thirst for knowledge did not enter this territory; perhaps she thought me a mythical being, and by discovering the truth about me, she would lose me. Well, yes. It was indeed something like that.

We welcomed the wonder of life in the most beautiful and challenging ways, us two, the young woman and her ageing teacher. But we also witnessed the cruel, cruel actions of mother nature and how it broke the hearts of women everywhere. With each baby we had to bury, with each mother who sacrificed her own life for the one inside of her, Nevena wept. I understood all of this and I explained to my girl; it was the sisters Vesna and Morena, the givers and takers of life, whose seemingly unpredictable motives were in fact very cyclical, therefore predictable, and necessary in understanding the true value of life. Love comes at a cost; it is grief. 'I will never love anyone then.' Nevena proclaimed, in a rare revelation of her youthful naivety.

Oh, my *devojka*. When it comes to love, you will have no choice.

Celebrations were held in the village we had just left, after the successful delivery of triplets. Nevena was simply masterful. She read all the signs as though she could see directly through the mother's skin and into her womb, calculating each exact movement and position, engaging every contraction and empowering the mother to do the most miraculous thing of all. The three small but healthy babies were immediately blessed, and the villagers thanked Nevena endlessly, inviting her to join them in their celebrations. But she politely declined, and we retired to our caravan, ready to move on to the next woman who needed us.

I knew my time with Nevena soon had to end. I had just seen her at the pinnacle of her work, and after the delivery of the third baby, I saw there was no more I could do for my *devojka*. She knew it all, and her purpose had been realised. There required no more weaving and threading, no more intervention and gentle realignment of trajectories.

'Three babies is a blessing indeed,' Nevena commented. 'But this mother will have her hands full! I hope her community remembers this, even after the celebrations end.'

'I am hopeful that she will receive the support she needs,' I replied. 'She had a strong family around her and an untypically supportive husband. That in itself is miraculous!' I chuckled, and Nevena gave me a half-smile. But a shadow lingered across her face and I could see anguish in her eyes.

'Nevena?' I said, drawing her gaze up to meet mine. Maybe I had spoken too soon. Maybe this young woman desired something more than just this. How could I have been so ignorant? How could I have thought that somehow, I would be enough for her?

'You wish for a family, do you not?' I asked.

'I wish for the impossible.' Nevena replied flatly.

'Impossible? What nonsense,' I said. 'Any man would trip over his own feet to get to be with you and to bless you with a family. Whatever man you desire, he will be yours.' I was sure that in this area, Nevena would require no interference on my part. She had a magic all her own that was purer than anything the Goddesses could procure.

'But that's exactly the problem,' Nevena whispered. 'I don't desire a… man. I do not desire *men* at all.'

Ah, but of course.

Of course, of course. There was destiny again, always a step ahead and with other plans in mind. I nodded my head and understood.

'Do not fear,' I said to my Nevena. 'Love is not found in a man. Even the women who desire men will be able to tell you that. You will know true love when you feel it.'

I said no more and left Nevena to rest. I watched her fall asleep as I sat in the chair beside her bed, gently weaving a thread between my fingers.

Nevena and I continued our work unperturbed, my *devojka* giving no indication that our conversation had seared itself into her mind, although I knew it had. She worked with a newfound resolve and imparted a little of her love onto every child she helped welcome into this world.

Until one humid and overcast morning, we found a letter slipped under the door of our caravan. *Please come immediately. My baby's life is in your hands.*

Wasting no time, we followed the directions to a modest dwelling nestled deep into the shrubbery on the outskirts of the largest neighbouring town. It looked uninhabited, but as we approached the front door, a young woman opened it and ushered us in quickly, glancing left and right before shutting the door behind us.

Inside, it smelled of warm blood and sticky skin.

'The baby has been born already.' Nevena announced to the young woman, not needing to ask her at all.

'Yes, yes he has,' the young woman replied. 'He is asleep in the room next door. He is fine. And so am I.' She walked slowly, evidently having given birth very recently. She should still be resting, recovering. But she looked agitated.

'So, what is the issue?' Nevena asked, visibly confused. 'It's a boy.' the young woman said.

Lucky you, I thought. *And lucky him.*

'He is the son of the King. Illegitimate, of course.' The young woman spoke without shame, I was glad to see. But there was fear in her voice.

'When he found out I had fallen pregnant, he threatened to kill me and the baby. But I convinced him to show mercy. I said I had a feeling it was a girl. And if it was a girl, I would promise never to tell anyone whose it was and the baby would be no threat to him or his legacy.'

Nevena looked at the young woman with sympathy. She had kept it hidden, given birth alone, and then probably cried tears of both joy and sadness upon discovering her baby was a boy.

'You need to take him,' the young girl implored, staring directly at Nevena. 'I work for the King, I cannot leave here. I have so little, and even less to give.'

'That is an unbearably difficult thing to do...' Nevena began to say.

'I will tell him it was a girl. And that she did not survive. *Please.* If he sees the boy, he will kill him. I am sure of it.'

At that moment the baby let out a little cry, and Nevena went into the room next door, as though summoned by his voice. She picked up the boy and he stopped crying immediately. He took hold of her thumb with his little hand, squeezing his fingers around it.

I saw Nevena swallow hard, her eyes watering. I saw her fall in love.

We travelled further than we needed to, where we were perhaps less well known; where the black mountains parted to reveal the opening of the sea, and silver cliff faces cascaded downwards like steps, into endless navy blue. The salt air smelled of new beginnings. The pink horizon appeared endless.

And this time, I knew I had woven a complete story, and it was time to finish it.

Nevena found love not through a man, but a boy. She had become a mother not by her womb, but her heart. And there would be so much more love for her still to come.

'*Mokosh*,' she said to me through crystal eyes. It felt good to hear her say my name. It kept me going. I kissed her forehead, and then the boy's forehead. I saw his destiny already. His strength and kindness would be revered for generations to come.

Nevena, no longer my *devojka*. Now she was someone else's, but also her own; Woman. Mother. Goddess.

Chaos
Isabella Luna

I.
Silk cocoon
of time and
not-yet space.
Until   flesh
tears, births the
Universe.

We are light.
Phosphenes thread
together.

Ours is the
gossamer
becoming.
Violet
eruption
of crushed stars
and currants:
sonorous
syzygy.

II.
She is born. Hecate. *Heh-ka-teh*. The singed world sings newness like
a lullaby. The first stars, a first word. The first planets, a first step.
The first Gods, a stumble. A learning. Time is the pumpkin seeds
spilling between her fingers to the mortals far below. She is a young
Titan and therefore an old God. Justice in this world is swift and the
battles are eternal. Then the Olympians rise. Their Father God is
smaller than hers, though perhaps more powerful. There is rivalry
between Old Gods and New. Yet when the ichorous godblood finally
dries on the New face of Olympus, Zeus appears before her and
bows. 'I honour You, child of Destruction and Falling Stars. I honour
You above all.'

We grow. Cadenza and chorale, and always an ostinato antecedent. Fire and blood, a dark moon in an open mouth, spilling prophecies, ghosts, and storms. A key, a blade, a limb of blackthorn. So old you can smell Our burning stars. So young you can smell Our peppermint, just budding. Our blood Our blood Our blood thrumming. Listen. Listen to Our blood searing through the flesh of silence. Know Us. As a menagerie of beasts, a menagerie of woman. A chimera of sky, sea, and earth. Fig, almond, and olive. Crow, hound, and snake. We are a palm-full of teeth, pomegranate seeds, and caesurae. We are here, open.

I become. Monster. Body. Woman.

III.
somewhere, a body. split here, here, and
here.

somewhere, a light. ignites within and spills
beneath flesh in thirds. there is no exit wound.

somewhere, a sea. she,
because she is always a she, opens

everywhere, everywhere. all of her opens like
flowers   doors   closets   mouths—

[the gasp of breath after surfacing fills your ears. you are ready to
begin.]

The Goddess of Broken Promises
Rebecca Dale

The storm crept up on me. That's the problem of being a plaything for otherworldly beings. The world, your bills, your stomach; all these things are indifferent to your circumstances. The cogs of capitalism care only for their own mythologies.

There was a tension headache orbiting my skull that felt as ominous as my supervisor's deadline. So I made a single mistake, a drop in the sea of my constant vigilance. Thunder clapped so hard it made my desk reverberate. I looked up and knew at once what I had done. He was coming.

I rifled through my things as rain assaulted the windowpane. Somewhere in the labyrinth of my office was a protection stone. A back-up plan.

"It's been so long", he said.

His voice oozed like raw honeycomb, just like I remembered. "Are you avoiding me?" he asked. He was a shadow behind me, his breath coasting the line of my neck, and I hadn't heard a single footstep, even though the building was old and the doors always creaked in their frames.

"You use doors these days?" I asked. Despite how tightly I'd clenched my stomach, I couldn't get the panic out of my voice.

"Beautiful as ever," he said and brushed my hair over one shoulder. "I knew a nymph like you once. She too shunned combs and brushes, even when it grew so long it swept the floor when she walked. Dishevelled," he enunciated. "As if she had just come from bed. Beautiful bedroom eyes, just like yours. The way that she swooned in my arms, it's enough to make you-"

"We have a bargain", I said. My voice tremored over every syllable. Silence reigned first, but then he sighed and slipped around me. He dropped into the empty chair in front of my desk, his beard shining like spun sugar in the overcast light.

"Do you remember the night you promised me anything?" he asked quietly, as I walked past him and up to the windowsill, turning and pushing my back into it. I shivered, even though the room was heated through.

"Anything within my power," I corrected.

"Very specific for a seven year old," he said. He shot me a smile that should have been captivating, enticing. But it was the eyes that ruined the trick.

"I want you to find someone," he said.

"I'm a research assistant, not a personal investigator."

"And once again, I'm the only one who sees your potential. I need discretion. Important to keep this away from prying eyes. And everybody else under my dominion is…you know," he waved his hand nonchalantly.

"A minor?"

He frowned. "I really would have preferred you younger. But there's a sense of anticipation, isn't there? I see why people wait. I'll give you until the end of the Olympic Games. That's fitting, isn't it? One way or the other you honour me."

"That's," I counted the days in my head, "…barely a week."

"If you don't find her, then our bargain is finally settled. Then you never have to hear from me again."

"Find who?"

"My wife," he said. "My ungrateful, poisonous, disobedient wife."

I doubled down on stupid mistakes. I started to make them in reams. I broke into a ranger's office and filled up the boot of my car with a hi-viz vest and witches hats and waited until the witching hour to match.

At three in the morning, I cut off the artery of a suburban intersection from each side so I could have the crossroads all to myself. There was a cemetery nestled into one corner. The neglected tombstones peered up from over the federation-aged stone walls; the perfect place for some desperate and thoroughly unwise witchcraft.

I dropped my bundle of tools with a thud; a metal rod, an empty jar, white chalk and black charcoal. The tarmac, slick with rain, resisted my chalk-lines. I twisted off the lid of the jar and pilfered the graveyard's consecrated earth, carrying it over in batches until it covered my shoddy design. I pulled up the pdf on my iPad and started the ritual.

The wind picked up and bustled through me. Even with the bomber jacket pulled tightly against my body and a scarf wrapped three times around my neck, I shivered and dropped the rod. I snatched it back up in haste.

She appeared—too soon, in gradients. First, the doorway, a slip of shadow cut away from the rest of the universe. I stammered over the incantation as she materialised. Then the crown, crafted from the skulls of the dead. The eyes, last. She tested the strength of the circle. I recoiled as raw magic spun out from her in a wide, lazy circle that knocked me off my feet. My hand scuffed against the tarmac and left them dripping.

Stupid, she said, to which I could only nod in agreement.

I cleared my throat. "I seek the queen of calves and lilies, of sceptres and thrones and feathers", I said. "I beseech you, Hecate, lady of crossroads and gateways, tell me if the great lady has wondered your paths".

She smiled at me, the grin you give a child when they set their will against you. Her laughter melded to the wind and left new blood trickling down my earlobes, until it collected at the collar of my jacket. She lifted me into the air as if I was nothing at all, licking her lips. My lungs heaved from the pressure of suspension. I could feel life leeching out of my cells, agitated out of me by her power.

Foolish, she said as my throat cramped in on itself and I grew faint. My cheeks swelled with blood vessels bursting their seams. *Such an attractive thing like you, calling out in the dark to whoever will listen. There are far worse masters than me waiting out in the din.*

And then the rod in my hand erupted as thunder clapped in the sky. An arc of lightning split the clouds and collected in my hand. The magic between us shattered. I slumped to the ground.

I see, said the goddess, as she watched me heave. She stepped over my chalk circles as if they were nothing and put out her hand. Cold hands wrapped themselves in mine and hoisted me up.

Better to fulfil your bargain. The lady of lilies does not look kindly on those who draw her husband's eye.

This is not my business, she said, and then she was gone. The tarmac ruptured in her wake like impacted glass. I heaped away the earth to reveal the sigil underneath, the one my mother taught me to help find my keys. It had been such a stupid idea, and I yelled as much to the empty intersection, until my hands found something in the rubble.

I hauled back into the safety of my office and put my head down. My phone screen blared with emails about my report, which I ignored and left unfinished across excel files, OneNote and two draft emails. Instead, I spent the next three days poring through pictures on Google Images. I found answers in the early work of the Dutch Masters. The pomegranate was stolen from a different time, before farmers had the will and means to alter the nature of their fruits. This was not a pomegranate to withstand voyages across seas and oceans. I trusted my mother's spell. It was a key. But I didn't know the lock, or even how to turn it.

Using a bread knife I found in the kitchenette, I sliced up the desiccated husk and peered inside. The seeds turned to dust when I cut them from the rind. I turned to family spellbooks, every one that I had lovingly scanned and compiled. I found a list of fruits matched to correlations and epithets. In one slim volume, I found a warning about divine beings and their intentions, sharing a page with a recipe for lavender scones. I cross-referenced my descriptions and observations across encyclopaedias, journal articles and ancient texts. I summoned him and told him our bargain was over.

"You see?" I said and gestured vaguely at the broken fruit.

"This is your evidence?" he scoffed.

"It's not like I can cross the river myself," I said. "But I'm certain. You'll find her there."

"I charged *you* with the task of finding her. I find it hard to believe my daughter would harbour her stepmother."

It sounded exactly like the kind of thing Persephone would do.

"Have you spoken to your daughter recently?" That was as close as I dared to question his parenting. "Where else would it come from?"

"Is this your way of giving up? Without seeming too eager?" He pushed me up against the wall, burying his face into my neck. I could feel the full heat of him, and the static crackling over my clothes. "I'd much rather stay here with you," he murmured, pressing a kiss into the crevice where my neck met my jaw. "But I do need to find her. Appearance's sake. It's bad for my reputation. I can't go trouncing into kingdoms that aren't mine."

"It's never stopped you before," I said.

"Mortals don't count. Until they do. It's a grey area."

"Get off me," I said. Acid began to rise in my stomach. "I'll do it myself."

"Are you really willing to go so far to avoid me?"

"You did this on purpose!" I yelled. "You knew she was there. You thought I wouldn't dare to go."

I crammed myself back against the plasterboard and buckled my knees to slip out from under him. I stumbled and clipped the side of his shoulder on the way through. A strange elastic sensation hauled me back towards him. Something snapped. I looked down and the crook of my pinky finger held a slim chain. I frantically bundled it into my pocket.

"There is no slight between us," he insisted. " I will hold to our bargain."

"You prey on the weak" I bleated, "When we are small and we don't know fair from crooked."

Shadows flocked to him, gathering around his hands, his face, obscuring his eyes. Suddenly he was the magic man in the bed. I was seven years old, pulling the covers around myself and wishing it all away with every spell I'd overheard in my mother's kitchen.

 "You sound just like her," he said.

My second spell also went awry. Halfway through the incantation, I slipped through the floor. I drowned in a pool of bad water. Fingers wrapped around my throat and pulled me upwards.

 When I finally opened my eyes, I lay at the foot of a new goddess, her crown bursting with rotting fruit. Ice traversed into my cell walls, trapped by a layer of sodden clothing that stank like rotting corpses left in the water. A spiral of ash whispered into the air as she clenched her fist tight over my stolen pomegranate. Endless void stretched behind her, except for a throne made of strangely augmented glass; sand and human bone compacted over millennia. *Insolent little thing*, she said. *You dare to come here? I will stretch you atom by atom until you are screaming and agony only.*

She threw me across an emerging glass floor. I slid without resistance into three waiting mouths, the teeth white and monstrous and gnashing. They clawed my jacket to bits. Gravity pulled me into the lowest set of teeth.

But they spat me back out. The translucent floor hit my back, collecting my body, spit and the putrid water of the river Styx.

"She smells like him," said a man, who lifted me up by the hood of my tattered cloak. "Like your father. Curious. Isn't she too old? It's not his taste. And yet, do you see the eyes?" He thrust me towards the goddess as if I were a fascinating artefact.

"I seek the lady of secrets and calves and lilies and lovers turned into ashes," I babbled, "I seek the lady that burns the hearts of forbidden lovers, trysts and passions."

"What an incredibly foolish thing to seek," said the man. "He sent you here, I suppose. Beloved, do you know what this means?"

Snuff her out, said the queen of graves and harvests. *He cannot reign here. The time of goddesses has come again.*

"It's not what she would want", said the man, adjusting his crown, "And in some matters, my word is still stone."

I teetered through space, then water, before surfacing in foam, liquid and salt. Jagged rocks surrounded me. By the time I dragged myself up onto land, a valley's worth of cuts covered all the parts of me that were exposed.

She waited for me at the end of a pier forged in ochre rock. A horizon! Grey ocean meeting grey sky. I gulped in air as I hobbled the distance, stretching my lungs as far as they would go.

She offered me a silver cup, filled with a liquid that clung to the sides like honey. "Better than whisky," I said.

Sit with me. We were a perfect tea party; me and the goddess of jealousy. I sat down and readied myself for the inevitable judgements; the colour of my eyes, the suitability of my colouring to his preferences.

I thought all the witches of this world were dead, she said instead.

"Only some," I said.

Is that so? She asked. She looked up into the sky and pursed her lips. *It's been so long since I've been up there. Tell me.*

"Alright," I said.

62

I told her about the noisy pipe in my little office and the old man who always hogged the photocopier at the university library. She poured me another glass. I asked about the brew, so she told me the voids she had walked between worlds, the bees that inhabited the comb between, who gave up their fruits in trade for crystalline flowers she'd picked from an emerald ocean.

Excellent friends, she said. *Over-pragmatic, sometimes.*

"Is there anywhere you haven't been?" I asked in wonder.

There's always more. I have been running for a very long time. I knew he would find someone, who in turn could find me. What did he offer you? Love? Power? Money?

"Reprieve," I replied. "He wanted me." I steeled myself for the Hera of legends; she of jealousy, she of revenge.

So you struck a bargain. What are the terms?

"I said I would do anything else except that. I didn't know what anything else could mean. If I don't deliver you...then.... but that's fair."

Some bargains are given to us by sleight of hand.

I began to weep. I clamped my hands over my eyes to hide the tears. She put her arm around me, guiding me back along the pier, even as my feet stumbled and the waves crashed higher against the shoals. She wiped my cheeks with both hands. *I will not send you back empty-handed. We will go together.*

I found myself shaking my head. My arms slipped around her, presumptuous, blasphemous, the kind of behaviour that compels gods to dangerous magic.

"No, I'll yield," I cried.

And what poor innocent will be next, after you? Her lips formed a thin line, so full of rage I trembled at it.

"But you've endured him for centuries!" I said, "I've only had a lifetime."

My aptitude in this task exceeds yours, although there was a time when I bore it better. I was much stronger once. I was the goddess of earth and sky and stone. Now I am the goddess of shattered vows only.

The sky crackled. Her hand swung out, the fingers loose and grasping, holding nothing. She sighed. *Even that was mine, the weapon of the clouds.*

Something burned against my thigh, until I yelped to be free from it. I frantically reached into the sodden pocket that clung to my skin. I pulled out the chain, weighed down by the pendant. I dangled it between us. The air snatched it.

Where…where did you get that?

I couldn't answer because she was laughing, deep and rich and warm like a hearty fire, and I couldn't stop myself from laughing too.

I have a bargain, for you, little witch, she said, as I offered it to her freely. The sky crackled with light as it dropped into her palm. *Take it if you will, with open eyes.*

"Anything," he said, as if I didn't remember. "You said you would give me anything."

I shivered, in memory to old fears. Even outside in the field beneath my office window, surrounded by the morning frost, the heat of his breath licked my face.

I had so much to say, every word loaded with anger and sadness and fear. But I had learned a thing or two, in the span between worlds. Words were wasted on those who only knew to twist them. I put out both my hands, resting them on his collarbones. When the placement was just as she had demonstrated, I called down the unrelenting power of the skies.

Lightning forked through him in a perfect line. Dust and flame plumed from his skin. He fell to his knees. The wild-eyed look on his face! I stepped back to let him slump into the grass.

"Thief!" he croaked. "You stole it from me, you… you stole-"

"I borrowed it," I said. "And soon I'll return it to its true master."

He called me a thousand names. His hair began to come out in singed, silver clumps, tipped in blood. I reached into my jacket and pulled out a sealed envelope, dropping it into his lap.

"Divorce papers. Printed them myself."

"She is the goddess of marriage," he spat. "She cannot-"

"She's the goddess of promises," I corrected, as I zipped up my jacket and walked away, "And I pity those that give them in bad faith."

become / error
Eunice Anrada

[*NSW State Archives show a photograph of female inmates exercising in the grounds of the State Reformatory for Women, year unknown*]

to be seen under the
condition of silence
awaiting   inspection
stiff as coin-operated clockwork

to be hidden like the metal
skeleton of buildings limbs
raised like beams
embedded in daily
architecture

once   a man I thought
to be my equal chastised me
for not showing the shape of
my body

I occupied space and
did not leave
                a shadow

are you still a woman holding
steady against the light if you
are not called

                    error

denied the chance
for photosynthesis
a woman thrives in
dark corners

no other choice for

a body un-

surveilled   but to
become

Yama Uba
Romy Tara Wenzel

On the ninth day of winter, before the deep snowdrifts that chilled toes in their straw boots, the sons and daughters of the village took their oldest folk up the mountain. The procession inched up the dirt paths and cobbled stones, making frequent stops. Some elders used sticks as a third leg, thumping them with the determination of shamans calling for rain on the earth. Young, strong farmers carried the weakest on their backs in bamboo and wicker baskets like those used by mothers working the fields. The last grandmother in line, Mother Yurei, was too infirm to draw her legs up like a grasshopper. Two men pulled her on a sled instead.

The path was an old trail, used by hundreds from the village to make this same journey when the days shortened and the food supply dwindled. The tradesmen of the village cleared and repaired the path every autumn to ensure the safe passage of those who made the climb: filling in holes, removing tree roots, scraping down moss. Families took care that their parents wanted for nothing on the trail, ensuring their elders took rest and treats to keep their energy up. Mother Kaiso stopped to bite the sweet rice-cake in her pocket. The village granary was already running low, but each family kept aside an extra portion of rice to prepare mochi for this day.

"We must go to the very top, Mother," her son said earnestly, taking her arm. "If we cannot get to the highest point, the gods will not hear our prayers for your long life and happiness."

Mother Kaiso nodded the wrinkled head under her straw hat, but said nothing. At the top of the mountain, Mother Kaiso knew, there was no altar nor temple. At the top of the mountain was Yama Uba, and she would be waiting for them. Mother Kaiso had taken her own parents there, forty winters ago, although she tried not to think about that too much.

There was a cry behind them, as one of the women slumped over like a rotten post. It was the tatami-maker's mother, and her son Kanoba rushed to her side, crying his mother's name. The village steward, who always accompanied the pilgrims, kneeled by them and checked the woman's breath.

"Her kami has left her," he declared. Kanoba hung his head, burying his face in his hands. To bring his mother up the mountain was a final rite of passage. Losing an elder on this journey brought ill-luck on their family for four generations.

The village steward looked up, and tiny snowflakes caught in his chin whiskers.

"There is nothing to be done," he said. "Leave her. We'll put her on the sled on the way back." Kanoba nodded and followed the steward's stride. The slow procession began creeping up the slope again. No-one mentioned how Mother Yurei would get down the mountain, if they were to use her sled for the corpse.

They entered a mist and emerged from the other side, scarves beaded with dew. A shadow passed over their heads, and the travellers tilted their straw hats back.

"A Yatagarasu!" cried Kanoba, as the bird keeled round in a circle lower down the path. "It has come to steal Mother's kami!"

"It's just a crow," his friends reassured him. "It had two legs, not three, and is hunting a rabbit or vole." But Kanoba could not be consoled, and although he continued to walk behind the others, his eyes did not stop streaming, his tears making prints in the light snow on the ground.

At the top of the mountain was a little hut with a round door, cradled by a half-moon of fir trees. Next to the cabin was a neat pile of wood with a hatchet buried in a bolt of pine. Rabbit and salmon skins hung on a line by a fire, and smoke rose from the chimney that nested into the shingled roof.

The children stood back, not knowing what to do next. Their parents, who had seen all this before, filed beneath a thick rope twisted from rice straw that hung from a joist above the round door. The last service they could do for their children was to go quietly and without complaining. Yet none of them had the courage to knock.

Yama Uba emerged not from the house, but from the forest. The Yatagarasu was perched on her shoulder, a glassy-eyed fox hanging limp from her hand. Her hair was the colour of smoke and she wore it twisted on top of her head like a warrior. She had a white deerskin around her shoulders and turned fur boots on her feet. As she crossed the fresh snow, she did not leave any footprints behind. The children of the elders drew back in fear, stumbling in the snow.

Several elders let unwilling cries escape their crinkled lips, but others sat up straighter and set their few good teeth together, refusing to look away.

Yama Uba did not express surprise or greeting at the small crowd of people, but ignored them altogether. She laid the fox out on the table and bound its feet with hemp. The muscles in her jaw bulged as she concentrated on her knots, and looked very good for grinding meat. Some elders shivered, and some of the young people as well.

Yama Uba strung up her fox in the rafters, clapped three times, and murmured a few words. Then she passed under the twisted hank of rope at the threshold, opened the door, and waited.

The elders filed inside, some casting painful glances back at their families. Mother Kaiso did not look back at her son. She remembered how it been, that look as the round door closed, fear widening her mother's eyes. She did not want her son to live with that, and would rather bear her burden alone.

One of the women ran forward after her mother. Yama Uba stopped her with her hand.

"You may not pass under the Shimenawa," she said, indicating the rope. "Only the oldest generation may do that."

Yama Uba cackled as she closed the door. She listened as the children of the old folks wept fatefully, and the crunch of their footsteps in the thickening snow died away. She turned to look at the old people, huddled together by the warmth of the fire. She went to a corner of the room, and scattered cushions stacked unobtrusively in a corner.

"Sit down," she said.

Yama Uba took the iron kettle from the stove, filled it with stand-water, and put it on the fire. The old people shivered, wondering if Yama Uba was beginning the broth for the stock-pot, to boil down the marrow from their bones. But they took the seats she offered; they had not run in too many years, and they might fall and shatter like clay if they tried. Yama Uba watched the fire, her face folded into a thoughtful frown. When the kettle sang, she picked it up with a cloth and poured out cups of hot chrysanthemum tea with the flowers in.

As the light faded, Yama Uba took blankets, tablecloths and shawls from her linen closet, and wrapped them around the shoulders of the old folks. She put rice-paper frames into the windows as the insects woke outside, and lit the sardine oil lamps. Mother Kaiso watched Yama Uba do this with her eyes half-closed, like a cat. Unlike those already reclined, she did not trust Yama Uba enough to sleep, no matter how weary her old spine. If Mother Kaiso was to be prepared in a soup, she wanted to know about it.

The flower opened in her tea, and she put it to her lips. The wild chrysanthemums on the mountain had a different flavour to the ones grown in the village plot; herbal and sweet.

Yama Uba stoked the fire, went to a cupboard and pulled out some ancient rolls of tatami.

Mother Kaiso inhaled the sweet rush as she lay down, feeling her hips creak and open. The weave had compressed over time, but the tatami was clean and good. Mother Kaiso had not smelled tatami so fragrant since her childhood, when she travelled to make offerings at the Izanami temple with her parents for the sister she lost.

Yama Uba was an old person herself, Mother Kaiso supposed, although no older than when Mother Kaiso had last seen her, forty years ago. Witches stopped growing at a certain age, or could give the illusion of it. Mother Kaiso would have liked that gift. She preferred the company of the young girls in the village, who joked and gossiped and played games while they worked, but while the young ones cooked and cleaned Mother Kaiso was obliged to pick over rice grains and listen to old women complain of endless ailments.

When Mother Kaiso opened her eyes the next morning, a black thing was sitting on the face of the woman next to her. Mother Kaiso leapt up, her knees cracking, and shooed the three-legged crow away. The bird stretched his wings and quarreled, and the woman herself sat up, yawning.

"Are you alright, Himari-san?" Mother Kaiso asked the woman, who was looking around as if woken from a dream. "That Yatagarasu was eating your eyes."

"My eyes are better than ever," Himari said, in wonder. "I can see you clear as day, Kaiso-san. Your hair is beautiful, like silver. I thought it long turned to snow."

Mother Kaiso squinted at Himari's eyes, and saw that the thick cataracts had cleared. For the first time in thirty years she was reminded of Himari as a young girl, her unusual eyes the colour of almond wood.

"Kojiki has no taste for eyes," Yama Uba said from the doorway, and the raven flew to her hand, grasping her knuckles with his three feet. "He just likes things tidied up. And if you don't want spirits moving into the bathroom, you best get scrubbing, Kaiso-san," she said, making the sign against demons. "There are plenty of akaname out there waiting for a filthy bathroom to maul with their tongue."

Yama Uba made them salt cabbages, smoke fish, fetch kindling, chop firewood, prepare winter greens. She spared no fingers that could bend. When hands could not work, Yama Uba found a way for them to be useful. Mother Yurei's joints were clawed from boro work, so Yama Uba set Himari to winding skeins of wool around Mother Yurei's splayed fingers.

Mother Kaiso smiled to watch them. They reminded her of the village children playing ayatori with strings.

"We are too old and frail for such work," said Chiyo, one of the worst complainers in the village. Yama Uba turned burning eyes on her, her mouth sour.

"If you are well enough to be out of bed, you must help with the chores," Yama Uba said. "That is the way of things around here. Are you no longer useful to me, Chiyo-san? That is good to know." She put a large pot of dashi stock on, and Chiyo got to scaling fish in a hurry.

The others worked just as hard, cleaning, keeping the fire going, tending the sick folks, preparing vegetables for dinner. They ate together, with warm coals underneath the table and blankets over their creaky knees. Then Yama Uba would go out by the last light to make her devotions to the forest kami, and the women would drink tea and gossip while she was gone.

"She enjoys having servants," grumbled Chiyo. A chrysanthemum petal caught on the hair of her lip, and she flicked her tongue over it like a mamushi viper. "When we can't do her dishes anymore, she will put us in her dashi stock for sure."

"But she does not eat the folk too sick to work," Mother Kaiso
pointed out. "She feeds and tends to them as if they were her own
parents. And she does not give us any task she does not do herself."
This was true, and Chiyo did not say any more, but sipped her tea
through lips thin as a bamboo leaf.

Curiously, Mother Kaiso enjoyed the company of the older folk at
Yama Uba's more than before. The men, who at home had sat
outside playing shogi, stoked the fire and carried wood, and one or
two even had a go at the hatchet after they saw Yama Uba doing it.
The women, who had been busy all day long complaining of their
aches, pains, and the laziness of their children, occupied themselves
with work that kept their hands busy. Mother Kaiso stitched the rice
straw boots that had frayed on the walk up the mountain. Some of
the other old folk repaired tatami in a corner, while the others
cleaned and sliced the dried meat Yama Uba had brought in from
smoking. Kojiki sometimes stole a piece, but the women only
laughed and teased him, telling him he would grow a third wing if
he ate so much.

But they were all old, and over winter, some died. Yama Uba had the
women wash
and wrap each body, and the men carry it out to her little
wheelbarrow outside. Then she went to the northern forest, and did
not come back for one day and a night.

Chiyo swore she could smell roasting meat on the wind, when Yama
Uba disappeared with her wheelbarrow into the trees. Yama Uba
had gorged her fill, Chiyo suggested, and any flesh she could not
finish she offered to demons in the forest heart. Evil things lurked in
there that attacked lone travelers: human-eating centipedes,
rainbow-breathing ogama toads, and blooded akateko hands.
Otherwise she, Chiyo, would have run away long ago, she said,
because she still had the legs of a girl, and they would carry her back
all the way to the village, if it were not for the demons on the road.

By the time the winter had passed, so had half of the old folks. Yama
Uba bundled their bones with their belongings, and left them at the
shrine halfway down the mountain. Their families wept when they
found parcels of their relatives at the halfway shrine. They took the
bones back to the village, put them in larch boxes, and wrote prayers
in beautifully inked script to hang above the relics. They bemoaned

the heartlessness of Yama Uba, who ate their ancestors, and commemorated their passing with a feast, a portion set aside for the one passed over. After the ceremony, their duty done, they put away the portraits, and ate the food themselves.

Kanoba, who still remembered the expression on his mother's face when she passed from being to non-being, was half-relieved as the bones started coming down the mountain. He might have been cursed for four generations, he said, but at least his mother had been saved from Yama Uba's wickedness.

saint audition
Eunice Anrada

their mothering frozen in plaster
eggshell-coloured saints
cradle lambs   skulls   bibles

the dust settles over sixteen versions
of the same woman her narrow face
and a-cup breasts

cloned across eight pews
they look down on the shadows
crawling to the altar

after reading poems in public a
sparkling redhead comes up to me
to say my words were so beautiful

and so feminine congratulating me on my
performance
in war the saints did not touch

even when this church
was a coral rock bomb shelter
suspended between

heaven and asphalt I might want
to be one of them untouched

by anything but light without prayer
I step outside reach for a body
closest to mine

Ruins
A. B. Young

As ghosts they still dance in the spring grasses: limbs extended in rapture, breaths held in fear.
They did not die all at once.

Perhaps you have heard this story told another way. They dance, sometimes, with demons until their shoes are danced-through. Other times, they are six sons. They become swans.
I tell you now: there were twelve and they drove their father to madness; twelve daughters dead, but not one gone.

The eldest, Ailís, drowned in the lake. Her foot caught the rotting boards of a sunken rowboat. The nails flaked against her flesh, her breath giving out only after the cold began to seep in.
It was the morning after the equinox. The blush pink skirts and orange curls became the sculpted curves of coral.
When he spoke in mourning, her father called her, 'My first love.'

The next year, Máire impaled herself. With laughter tripping from her lips, she chased her lady's maid through the woods, and did not see the tree branch in the morning fog. Her maid's scream mingled with birdsong and echoed for days.

The stepmother considers the ghosts a vicious punishment. They were not her intention. She wonders if some bestial deity heaped a law of threefold returns. It does not occur to her that, perhaps, she should never have attempted to utilise powers she does not understand. After all, rarely do the folk in these tales consider the consequences of magic.
The house is cavernous and stone, and silence gusts down hallways. She moves like ink as it smudges: smooth and fading out. She lingers behind corners.
The house is not hers.
Her husband sits in councils with advisors and ignores them. He taps a browning nail against a splintering windowsill. He taps the

tempo for a flute player long dead. There has not been music since Ailís.

The house, to him, is four walls.

Each year the deaths became more violent.

Brighíd was lost to an unseasonal blizzard. The following day, when the wind had soothed to a murmur, her father's men tracked sodden fields, calling Brighíd's name. The air still smelled of wet grasses and sweet woodsmoke.

They found her staring at the sky, eyelashes tipped in frost.

No one has entered the mirror room for several springs. It is where they converge, when they don't dance through hallways like sheer fabrics grazing stone walls. The sisters converse as if they are alive. The servants whisper that, perhaps, they do not know they are dead. Máire asks Saoirse if she may borrow her yellow dress, flitting from one mirror to another, cold glass painted as cold skin.

The room is twelve sides, a mirror on each wall. The girls used to stand in the centre and watch themselves multiply. Keely called it creation, the way their dresses layered—sprawling colour, bright and never ending—in the glass.

They practiced their dancing in preparation for spring equinox. Their shoes tattered against stone. All dead, they continue to practice daily.

It should be said that she thought she was protecting them. Many stepmothers in these tales are susceptible to jealousy, or a coldness of heart. She, however, loved her husband's daughters as fiercely in their deaths as she had the day she met them.

Saoirse complimented her, she remembers—asked, 'Will you teach us how to do such lovely braids?' and the other girls nodded. They crowded close to her chair before the hearth, twelve sets of cheeks flushed with excitement. Caitríona asked to examine the embroidery at the hem of her skirt. Morgan, who died six years later with a boar tusk in her leg, asked if she knew anything about hunting. Brighíd wanted to know what books she had brought with her, and if she could borrow them, for she'd read everything to be found in the house.

Each year, the stepmother watched the fear blossom in their pinched brows and tightening jaws as each winter thawed. The sadness was a corolla fissuring her chest.

Still, she does not know that she regrets the action that killed them. When the story is told as six sons turned to swans, it is said the king hides them away for fear of his wife's jealousy. He visits them weekly, skulking into the forest in unnecessary subterfuge.

The father's wife has known other men who hid their children from prying eyes.

Caitríona died trapped alone in the sewing room, gagging on grating smoke. The window panes smeared with soot. No one is sure how the fire started, or why it did not spread to the rest of the house.

The deaths followed the equinox. The third year, the sisters began to sleep that night together on the floor of the mirror room. They did not know in which order they would die. Fate, or misused magic as it were, seemed to snatch at opportunity rather than enact a plan. And so they piled the stone floor with pillows and blankets, high enough not to feel the sharp crevices where the tiles met. They curled into each other, whispered confessions and hurried forgivenesses multiplied by the mirrors.

Each equinox they danced with tears in their eyes, then held each other's hands until sunrise.

Keely and Úna were born together, but died a year apart.
Keely of sudden fever that flushed her skin and tore at her throat.

Nimah once suggested, as she and Úna kneaded dough, that they should not dance the equinox any longer.

'Don't be foolish,' Úna said, hushed. 'We danced for years before all this.'

The kitchen was a warm place then; smelling of dried rosemary and fennel, rushes strewn under bare feet. The girls were safe in that place for women. Even there, they did not speak of the deaths loudly.

Úna felt the growing child stretch in her womb, and rancid hate rose in her throat.

Keely, who stoked the oven fire, said, 'Imagine Deidre should hear you. Stop.'

Úna died in childbirth. There was no father to speak of. When the labour started the morning after the equinox, all knew what was coming.
The stepmother thought it a small mercy that the babe died too.

Little Deidre, the youngest sister, had a nightmare the night the stepmother cast her spell. Deidre burrowed into her side, sobbing. She had taken to sleeping in her stepmother's bed when the nightmares had begun to harrow her more than once a night.
Upon waking, her stepmother soothed her with soft songs and sure hands plaiting her curls. This night, though, her father came to his wife's bed and took Deidre away with him.
It was the barrenness of the girl's owl eyes that made the decision for her stepmother.

The usual way of things in these tales is that the mother died in childbirth. The sisters' mother hung herself among the paper reeds of the willow tree.
Many believed it was her vengeful spirit stealing the girls away each year—angered by the new wife whom her girls had so quickly come to love.
Their mother was not strong enough in death to complete such a task, after a life like hers.

Most days in late spring, Ailís and Léan took Deidre to watch the swans. Léan weaved crowns of grey flowers for her youngest sister. She shore the pin thorns and magicked them with delicate, raw fingertips among poppies and daisies.
The swans amassed close to shore, and when they dipped their beaks to drink their necks hooked gracefully.
Deidre did not make a habit of calling Ailís 'mama', but sometimes, on these days by the lake, she whispered it into her own orange curls. 'Mama,' she said, 'I would like to be a swan.'
Ailís didn't ask why. She had wished for the same thing, on occasion.

It was the eighth year that Saoirse took a glinting knife to her own skin.

'Fear is tiresome,' she said to Róisín, before she left the mirror room, kissing each of her four living sisters in turn.

Léan, Nimah, and Róisín died on the sixth, seventh, and ninth years. Léan was thrown from her horse; Nimah tumbled down a flight of stone stairs; Róisín ate something that swelled her throat until she could no longer breathe.

The year after all twelve daughters had gone, their father's rage reminds his wife, strangely, of the spell itself.

She had not known much of magic, only that certain objects and ideas hold more power than others: blood, places where deaths have occurred, repeated words, objects of sentimental value.

She knows far more of magic now.

In the reeds of the willow, she wiped bright blood from her own slashed palm onto the quilt that had covered her bed since childhood. The faded strips of colour wove a pattern of knots. They had failed to protect her, too.

She asked that he never be able to touch the girls again.

On her way back into the house at dawn, she passed the mirror room. The high windows cast bright light from one mirror to another and refracted a spectrum of colours across the room.

She stopped to watch the way it seemed to dance, and thought of swans taking flight.

This moment is what her husband's rage reminds her of. She savours it.

Deidre died last. Her father crushed the pillow over her face, hands holding the full weight of his body.

That night, she had danced the equinox alone, grass staining her bare ankles. Her orange curls swung behind her, heavy in braids done by her stepmother.

Their eyes had met in the mirror with the sturdy fingers tangled in Deidre's hair. Her stepmother said, 'You are so loved. And I am so sorry.'

Deidre understood, then. She could not find it in herself to be angry. Eleven sisters gone, eleven years of loss. It would be over soon for her, but not for her stepmother. She kissed her stepmother's cheeks. After her dance, her maid whispered, close to her ear, that she looked just as Ailís did at seventeen. She smiled, but the corners of her mouth felt heavy.

As she walked alone to the mirror room, her sisters' footsteps chased her through the passageways. Their voices were shouts from across a chasm. They told her they loved her, that they could not wait to hold her hands again.

She fell asleep, as she did every year, to their golden singing. It was not a song they had sung before their deaths. In it, the brothers who turned to swans became human again at the end.

When later she awoke to her father's footfall, her sisters could not protect her, and she knew she would not see the day ahead. She fought.

After, her father panted through animal sobs and his twelve daughters watched him from the mirrors. They did not duplicate in death, and Keely called this ruins.

They took turns to remind their father of his crimes, uttered one by one, like the creak of door hinges and the wind through roof thatching.

Their stepmother stays, because they do.

Beloved of Our Beloved
Raksha Muthukumar

"Radhe Radhe! The word resonates from every street corner in the town of Vrindavan, where Radha eternally lives. Forgetting our names and the bindings of our lives, upon hearing Krishna's flute we instantly transform into Radha, the beloved of our beloved, the secret lover within."

Jai Uttal

"Radha! Radha, are you coming?"
Radha looked up from the clothes she was pushing over the washing stone. She wiped a hand across her brow and squinted up at her best friend on the riverbank.
"Arey, Naina, what do you think?" Radha retorted, gesturing at her attire, well-worn from the long day of chores. "Looking like this? I'm not going anywhere except straight home!"
Naina laughed as she looked her friend up and down. Radha's hair was disheveled in its braid and her sari was knotted at her calves to keep its hem out of the water. Her friend's hands were red from the soap and vigor of her washing and her body showed her fatigue. Despite that, Radha's eyes were twinkling in amusement at her friend's obvious excitement.
"Radha, the chores will still be here tomorrow. Hurry, before we become old maids," Naina tugged at her hand.
Radha sighed as she freed herself from Naina's earnest grasp. "No, Naina, not tonight. I'll join you and the girls next week, I promise."
"You say that every week, Radha," Naina pointed out.
Radha smiled wryly at her friend. "One day, it'll even be true, Naina. Patience, we're not old maids yet. Now come help me put these clothes in the basket before you head into the woods."

"Where are your thoughts tonight, beloved?"
Radha lay with her eyes closed and her head in her husband's lap as he stroked her hair gently behind her ears. Ayan leaned against the wall of the veranda as the pair enjoyed the quiet nighttime air. The crickets chirped in the cool night as the cicadas hummed their response. These were the moments Radha cherished the most.

She opened her eyes and looked out across the field and up at the stars. Despite having never traveled outside Vrindavan, Radha knew in her heart that the sky overhead was the most beautiful in all the world. She found Chithra and Rohini   in the sky and followed their twinkling points until they led past the place her eyes could behold. "I was thinking of Naina. She came to me while I was finishing the wash today to invite me to the woods with the rest of the village girls."

"And?" Ayan prodded gently. He always knew when his wife's mind was heavy with troubles and Radha was reminded again of the luck she had to call this patient and compassionate man her husband.

"And-- nothing," Radha said, flustered. "Why should I join them in their song and dance?
I hear them laughing every night as the cowherd boys play their music."

"Wouldn't you like to laugh with them, Radha?"

"I find my merriment here, in our home, Ayan. I paint the rangoli and cherish the gardens that bring us sweet smells and colors. I read books and share their stories with you at night. What is wrong with wanting the contentment that is here instead of the one that is over there?"

Her husband was silent as he thought.

"Radha, no one is diminishing the joys you already hold dearly by introducing new ones. Your rangoli will not lack in beauty because you begin to enjoy song and laughter with your friends. There is no betrayal in opening our hearts up to something more to love; indeed there is no point when we become so full that we have to push something else out. Do not fear change in this life for indeed change will come whether we want it to or not."

Radha pulled her husband into a tight embrace and held onto him the way she wanted to hold onto this night. She looked up at the stars and wished she knew as confidently as they did what tomorrow would bring.

"What? Who's this? Radha has come down from her abode tonight to join us mortals?"

The gopis teased good naturedly as Radha appeared through the brush.

"Hush, now, you lot," Naina rolled her eyes at her companions. "You're just jealous that she's here to dance better than all of you." Radha laughed as she embraced her best friend. While the idea that anyone would be jealous of her dancing struck her as absurd, she was nonetheless heartened by Naina's zealous defense. She took a deep breath and relaxed into the company of her old friends. Just a short while, she thought.

Radha tied on her anklets as she listened to one of the girls regale the group with stories of her small child. Apparently he had broken a clay pot of cream before unabashedly eating half of it. The peals of laughter in the group rose and fell just as quickly and Radha turned to see what had caused the sudden hush.

Her gaze fell on a slim dark-skinned young man arriving in the clearing. As Radha looked at him, she could not pinpoint anything extraordinary about his appearance, and yet she felt as though she couldn't tear her eyes away. He had the build of most of the farmhands and cowherds of the village and a smile that seemed as mischievous as it was bright. He wore a yellow lungi and a peacock feather in his long midnight hair and he arrived with a flute held in his hand. Radha was immediately aware of what brought the girls from the village to the woods each night.

"Krishna," the gopis cried, excitedly. They clambored for his attention and Radha could only stand back and look on bemusedly as Naina shrugged her shoulders as if to say, what? I told you this would be fun.

She watched the young man flirt back shamelessly with each of the gopis in turn. He complimented the jewels in their hair and asked about their families. He touched their hands and looked into their eyes, and Radha could see even from a distance that they all caught their breath when that happened. He effortlessly moved between them as he twirled his flute.

Eventually the cowherd noticed Radha's presence. His face broke into a crooked grin that instantly made Radha feel suspicious. "And who invited you here tonight, beautiful one?" He asked her teasingly.

"I'm Radha. Naina invited me tonight. Every night, really, until I relented."

"Oh? And what kept you away from us for so long?" Krishna inquired.

"I'm here now, aren't I?" Radha said. "I was lured on the promise of song and dance."

Krishna's smile was beatific. He bowed to her with a twirl of his hands. "And you shall have it, lady," and he raised his flute to his lips.

It had been several weeks and Radha had begrudgingly started attending the festivities in the woods regularly. Her husband was right, her new nighttime activities had only added to the other parts of her life. She found herself humming the songs from Krishna's flute as she painted the veranda with chalk dust.

"What is that song, Radha?" Her husband asked one day when he returned from his teaching duties.

"Krishna, the cowherd, played it on the flute last night," Radha replied. "I cannot forget its beauty."

Ayan smiled. "And now I cannot either. It is indeed enchanting."

"Ayan," Radha said suddenly. "Is Shrishti's daughter in your class? Her name is Laila."

"Yes, Laila is in my class. Why do you ask, Radha?"

Radha shrugged. "Shrishti never stops talking about Laila. It might be pleasant to have them over one evening for tea and snacks."

Ayan looked surprised but pleased. "Yes, my dear, that would indeed be nice." He kissed her cheek and walked towards the doorway before pausing. "You know, you've changed since you started dancing with the girls regularly."

"Dear husband," Radha smiled ruefully. "Is it really that strange for me to invite a friend over?"

"Of course not," Ayan held his hands up in a placating gesture. "I only mean… well, you've brought music into our home. You ask after my students and befriend their mothers. You've been sleeping well and waking with a smile on your face. It brings me such joy to see your light brighten, Radha."

"The cowherd who plays the flute each night is gifted, Ayan," Radha confessed. "He makes us want to dance and sing and forget all our troubles. I feel restored and as if everything in
the world is as it should be when Krishna plays."
"Then, my love, I hope he never stops playing for you."

"What did you think of that last song?" Krishna asked her one night. Radha stopped and considered. "It was upbeat and the rhythm made my heart pound, but I think I prefer when we end on something more melodic. It brings a sense of calm before we all go home for the night."
Krishna nodded and considered her suggestion. He slowly raised his flute and played a gentle melody without breaking eye contact with Radha.
Radha ignored the looks from the other girls and the lump in her own throat.
"What was that?" She asked softly when he finished.
"It was a lullaby. My mother used to sing it to me when I was a child." Krishna's expression was contemplative. "Did you like that better?"
"I did, thank you." Radha returned his gaze steadily. Something about Krishna made her feel like she was back in school answering a teacher's difficult question. She stood with her spine ramrod straight and spoke as if guarding against one slip that would lead to her downfall.
"Good," he smiled easily. "I'll be sure to end our nights together like that from now on. Thank you, Radha."
And with that, Krishna of Vrindavan walked out of the woods as if nothing had happened.

"Radha and Krishna sitting in a tree--" Naina sang the next day as she and Radha drew water from the well.
Radha rolled her eyes and the other women at the well laughed. "As if you can talk. You didn't tell me the real   reason you girls go to the woods every night."
"What do you mean?" Naina asked innocently. "Krishna plays the flute so beautifully, you can't help but to dance to it."
"Yes," Radha said sarcastically. "Krishna's… flute."

The girls all laughed and Radha permitted herself a small smile as she walked back towards her home. If her thoughts wandered to a certain dark-skinned man, well then it was because Naina had brought him up.

"Hey, Radha!"

Radha turned towards the fields and abruptly stopped in her tracks.

Waving at her from the pastures was none other than the man himself, as if summoned from her thoughts. Krishna stopped his waving and jogged over to her, a smile wide across his face.

"Radha, I was just thinking of you," he said. He stood before her smiling boldly and

Radha raised an eyebrow.

"And I was thinking about the books my husband bought from the peddler yesterday," she said.

"Aren't you going to ask me what I was thinking about?"

"Aren't you going to ask me what my books are about?"

Krishna laughed. "I was thinking about how radiant the Yamuna River looked this morning and I was wondering if you or she were the most beautiful creation belonging to Vrindavan."

"The Yamuna doesn't only belong to Vrindavan, Krishna. It doesn't even start or end here."

"Just as you don't only belong to me," he answered swiftly. "But does that mean I cannot see the beauty of either one?"

"So will you not ask about my new books at all, then?" Radha said, deftly side-stepping the question. "If that's the case, I really must get this water back home."

Krishna stepped out of her path and gestured gallantly for her to continue on her way. "I did not ask you about your books because I did not want to hear about them when I could experience them firsthand," he said to her retreating back. "Bring them to the Yamuna tomorrow morning so I can hear you reading them aloud."

She ignored the flip of her stomach and snorted at his audacity. "In your dreams, Krishna!"

Radha put the water pail down more forcefully than she intended, making her husband jump.

"My God, what did that water do to you, Radha? Tell me so I can be sure to never do the same," he joked.

"It's nothing," Radha replied, scowling. "It's just… the cowherd, Krishna, who plays the music for the girls every night. I find him troublesome."

"Do you?" Ayan asked. He put down his papers and rubbed his chin thoughtfully. "You have never seemed troubled when you come home from dancing."

"He's maddening. The other girls tease and cajole him and he replies in riddles. I don't understand him at all!"

Ayan was looking more perplexed by the minute as his scholarly mind sought the source of his wife's vexation. "Is it how he treats the other girls? Did he say something to upset you?"

"Yes!" Radha burst out. "The vain man asked me to read to him on the Yamuna tomorrow morning. Can you imagine?"

"Ah."

The couple sat in silence as Ayan considered and Radha fumed. "Radha," Ayan began gently. "Are you upset because you do not want to do that, or because you do?"

Radha turned to her husband in shock and Ayan laughed softly. "I swore on the day I married you that my wife would never want for anything I could give her. What kind of a man would I be if I broke my vows so easily?"

For the second time that day, Radha swallowed a lump in her throat caused by looking upon a man she loved dearly.

Krishna whooped when he saw Radha walking down the river bank the next morning. He grasped her hands between his own.

"You may not believe me on this day, or even on our last day, but no matter what has come before or what will come after, the world will speak of the love between Radha-Krishna until its very last day. I'm very happy you came, beloved."

The whole universe yearns for Krishna but he yearns for Radha. Throughout India and the world their names are praised together-- Radhe Krishna, Radhe Krishna. Before Krishna arrived in Vrindavan, legends say Radha was indeed married to Ayan Ghosh. Some legends paint Radha's life outside of Krishna as joyless, and claim that the heartbreak of Krishna's departure from Vrindavan led her to taking her own life. Other regions tell the story of Ayan and Radha rekindling love after her heartbreak. After all, which pious husband could find his wife sinful for her devoted love and passion for a God? Krishna ascended the throne and married the princesses Rukmini and Satyabhama, and possibly many others, depending on the scripture consulted. The love between Radha and Krishna remained untarnished by the external obligations of marriage and kinghood. Their unconditional devotion to one another is worshiped as the purest form of selfless love, love that asks for nothing in return. And if you ask me, the love that Ayan bore for Radha should also be worshipped as such.

Human
Jaya Penelope

A poem for two voices

1. The dreamer

I dreamed a woman woven
of silver wire, her chest full
of space. I made her lustrous
and empty. When I laid my ear
to her breast I could hear the sea
sing where her heart would be.

I watched her walk away
over salt grey plains, looking
perhaps for something
to love, she found only the thin voice
of barbed wire winding
on hill tops.

2. The dreamed

I wish you'd wake.
I'm weary of the wind
tunnelling through the space
where my organs would be
if I were human.

I envy you your intimate
fortress of flesh.
I would dream myself
a body filled with a singing
tide, built of bone.

I know, I know, it's nothing
but a leaky parcel of flesh that aches

trembles, sinks particle
by particle back
into the earth, but oh-

the heavy pleasures of flesh licked
with sweat or goose-pricked cold
and of blood that seeps
where your skin is sliced
an eye that weeps salt
red tears, I tell you

if I were human
I'd never tarnish

first published in breath of the sea, 2012

The Long Boobed Ghost
Lieu Chi Nguyen

'And that's when I realised I had seen torch ghosts,' my grandma
finishes. I remember her voice is crackly like breaking palm sugar.
She pops a peeled lychee onto her tongue. Her leathery lips pucker
like the mouth of a catfish as she sucks off the cloudy flesh and spits
the pip into her hand and throws it into a wooden bowl.
Thock.

It is dinnertime and everyone else has started eating fruit. Only I am
left holding a rice bowl with braised pork. We have had this same
dish for the last three days after Grandpa slaughtered a pig for my
Great Sixth Aunt's Death Day Anniversary. I stare at the brown salty
cubes on the white rice grains and wrinkle my nose. With my small
ceramic spoon I scoop rice and bury the meat underneath. I'm sick of
pork.

I am the only child sitting on the *bo van nho* with my grandma, my
mum and Auntie Thu, around pits of lychees and rambutans.

There are two *bo van* in my family: a smaller one where me and the
women sit and a larger one where all the men, like Dad, Grandpa
and the Uncles sit. Each bo van is covered in a tam chieu. Both bo
van are in the lower house where the kitchen is. The upper house is
where we sleep and where the family altar is. Most of the houses in
Thu Duc before the war have leaf roofs but ours is made of tin
because my grandpa thinks tin is more durable. Later, it will protect
us from bullets fired by both armies. When I look up, I can see the
smoke stains from the firewood stove blackening the dull grey metal.
When I look down, under the *bo van* is a dirt floor that my mother
sweeps every day to stop our bare feet from getting dusty.

Out front is the rice paddy planted near a dirt road, which I was told
leads all the way to Saigon. My family's house sits within an orchard
of *trai mang cut, trai mang cau,* oranges and mandarins, which I'd help
my mother pick when in season. To the back, beyond the orchard, is

the family cemetery and behind that are sugar canes and coconut trees.

It is Summer and so the large metal doors of the lower house are wide open. Even though it's dark the air is still sweaty with heat and so only a few kerosene lamps have been lit. Black insects with wings buzz around the lights and the spirits of my grandma's words. This is the time when the men drink *ruou de* and smoke their pipes. This is the time when the women take turns to tell stories.

'Did you ever see the torch ghost again?' asks Auntie Thu, her voice like rustling bamboo.

Auntie Thu is one of the women who works in the rice paddy fields. I see her in the fields wearing her *non la* on her back, hanging off her neck by a purple cotton strap. She always forgets to put it on, which is why she has freckles on her face, unlike my mother's face which is pale and soft. My mother's skin is also clear whereas Auntie Thu's is warty, especially under her chin. The warts remind me of fire ant hills made of flesh. I remember my grandma telling me if I wanted my skin to be as *trang* as my mother's I should wash it with rice water. Back then there were no products like Olay.

Auntie Thu is my auntie but not in the way my mother and father's sisters are my *di* and *co*. Auntie Thu works for us and chews betel leaves with my grandma, who is my father's mother. Auntie Thu often has dinner with us because she lost her husband before she could have a baby. For some reason she never wanted to find another husband.

'Nope,' says Grandma swallowing another lychee. 'But there was that time with the strange rabbit...'

'Oh, I almost forgot,' interrupts Auntie Thu, her eyes wide and bulging as if she had *buou co*. She always got carried away with stories because she had no one at home to tell them to. 'Old Second Auntie Near Cau Bin Loi said her nephew saw the Long Boobed Ghost.'

Sitting with my back against the wall I stop burying my pork. I set my bowl on the *tam chieu* and look up. I have never heard of that ghost before. I have listened to my grandma's stories a thousand times. Grandma saw a lot of ghosts before she married my grandpa because she was a farmer's daughter and used to sell vegetables at the market. To do that, she would have to leave her house in the middle of the night. Ghosts only come out in the dark. Maybe my grandma tells so many ghost stories because now she stays inside all day cooking with my mother.

Auntie Thu sees me peering at her and bares her red stained teeth at me like a pregnant cat I once saw underneath the house. 'Nhi,' she says, 'If you're *hon* to your mother, or take her for granted by not eating the food she's cooked you, the Long Boobed Ghost will haunt you.'

I glance at my scrambled dinner and shrink sideways against the warmth of my mother, who is darning a pair of cotton pants by the light of the nearest kerosene lamp. Her shiny black hair is tied back from her face in a low chicken's tail. The lamp casts shadows on her high, white cheekbones. Her hands are bony, her fingers slim with skin so thin I can see the blue veins underneath. My mother's hands are unlike Grandma's and Auntie Thu's, which are as tough as chestnut shells. My mother's hands is soft and she is always doing something with them. If she is not mending our clothes, she is embroidering a handkerchief or crocheting fruit or flowers. My mother sighs, 'She has always been such a picky eater.'

'What's the Long Boobed Ghost?' I ask Auntie Thu as I pull my mother's hand from my head and clutch it, my nails digging into her veins.

Auntie Thu's eyes are sharp as metal knitting needles and pierce through mine. She bares her teeth again. 'The Long Boobed Ghost is the spirit of an old woman whose breasts are as long as zucchinis and as thick as *trai bi*. Her breasts are so long that if she had a baby on her back, it could reach forward, pull her breast towards it and

93

suckle from her nipple as she floats. If she sees that you have been rotten to your elders she will fly through your window at night and smother you with her bosom.' Auntie Thu leans closer to me until I smell a sickly mix of chewed fruit and stale breath, 'And I can tell you this, she lives in your sugar cane out past the graves.'

My eyes are as wide as my skin turns cold even in the sweaty heat of night. I look down at my bowl full of rice and pork. My stomach feels as if there are eels thrashing in it. There is silence then all the women around me laugh.

'Enough stories,' says my mother although I can see her eyes crinkle at the corners. 'It's time for you to go to bed.'

I hide my pout from my mother and climb off the *bo van nho*. As my feet touch the dirt floor I look out the back window. My neck prickles like there is a rambutan sitting on it. In the distance, I see the outline of the shadowy sugar cane field behind the cemetery. I stand up. My bum is sore and itchy from sitting on the *tam chieu*. Beneath the thin cotton of my cropped pants I can feel mat's ridges imprinted on my skin.

Later that night, I wake up to the sound of a mosquito. The insect repellent incense must have burnt out. I look around my room through the mosquito net that is suspended over my bed like a large, soft spider web. I look towards the wall to my left. My window does not have glass like the windows in Australia but is covered in metal bars that curve like an "S." These cast shadowy waves that loom like giant stick figures all over my bedroom walls. I swallow. My mouth is dry. My tummy grumbles. I realise I am very hungry. I turn away from the shadows. Maybe if I got up I could find my leftover dinner. Then, I see that outside my window the moon is almost full and reflects suspended tendrils of silver that looks like hair. Beneath those tendrils, I see the face of a woman with eyes glittering like black jade. My breath catches in my throat and I just stare and watch trying to breathe. On either side of the woman's jowly cheeks, her hands start to grip the windowsill with long, curved nails. Now I know what Auntie Thu was talking about.

The Long Boobed Ghost rises and glides through my window. She is squat and short and completely naked. Her skin is grey and wrinkled and sags like the matted fur of a feral dog. Her breasts, skinny and long as a zucchini but as fat as *trai bi* move closer and closer to my face as she descends. I thrash in bed, pushing up onto my elbows and back against my pillow. I still can't seem to breathe. Then her nipples, which are rough like bitter melon, enter my mouth and cover my nose. I try to take a deep breath to scream but I just suck more of her breast in. Her milk tastes like braised pork buried under rice. And now I'm not so hungry.

Lunch the next day is more pork and rice. I sit on the *bo van nho* with my mother and grandma and Auntie Thu. I dig in my ceramic spoon so I get all of the brown, gelatinous pork and white rice and eat and eat and eat. The saltiness of the pork and the lac taste of the rice blend with the sweetness of milk. I keep spooning until I finish eating before the women.

I feel Auntie Thu's knitting needle eyes on me. I turn to her. She looks at me, then my empty bowl, then back at my face. She bares her red teeth and chuckles, 'Did the Long Boobed Ghost whet your appetite?'

This story first appeared in Sweatshop Women (2018) published by Sweatshop: Literacy Movement Inc.

Unpicking Penelope
Jaya Penelope

On being named a Penelope;
I waited for years, in doorframes,
leaned fetchingly on windowsills
scoured the frilled edge of the ocean
my skirts billowing,
Scanned horizons for my lover
a tall ship, his hold full of oranges,
emeralds, sandalwood.

I had a feeling for those waily
Celtic laments where love's
patience is rewarded, persistence
martyred. I'd sing them to the sea;
bring him home to me
bring him home.

A maiden in aspic, pickled
in the vinegary fantasy of longing
I loved men with noses like the prows of ships,
navigators whose restless eyes charted distant seas.

Question:
What do men do when they leave the house?

The official answer:
*Sleep with sea nymphs, chase
anything made of gold*

What Homer didn't tell you:
After the waiting, the ten,
the twenty years of silence
when hope swung from the rafters
like ten hanged handmaidens,
Penelope slept with each suitor in turn.

In other versions she frolicked with some wild
god, gave birth to Pan.
I like to imagine her lying
in the greenwoods twined
with her goat-footed lover,

done with bed linen,
done with weaving,
with waiting
forever.

first published in Cuttlefish, Edition 1, April, 2015

In a Bed of Razorfish
KJ Mair

When is a house not a home?
You ponder this riddle as something hard hits you on the back of
your head. You fall face-first into the brine of the lake.
And sink.

It's your birthday and everything is fine, fine, fine.
Someone has thrown a party for you and you put on a smile, so
bright it deceives. Sometimes keeping war treaties and family
gatherings civil requires just the right number of teeth.
In the kitchen your mother is finishing the cake. Fluoro pink frosting
is piped over every square-inch of a mysterious-flavoured slab.
"Don't look! It's supposed to be a surprise."
Mum throws herself in front of the cake as if it were the president
and she the senior bodyguard. She attempts to shield your eyes with
a frosting-covered hand and you laugh and duck around her.
From up close, the cake looks as if Barbie has come to life and
decided to devote her miracle of sentience to decorating your cake.
It's very …
You frown. "Aren't I a little too old for this?"
Just for a second and so fast you think you're imagining it, her smile
fractures like a video game glitch. For a moment you think someone
else is smiling at you. Someone else using your mother's face.
But it's your mum. Just Mum.
"No one is ever too old for pink!"
You feel something inside you grow smaller.
"Of course not."
Remember, everything is fine.

They've drained the lake. Fish flip-flop and drown in the air. Mud
stinks when it's baking in the sun. You long for the easy breath of
salt. Funny, you swear you can taste it at the back of your throat.

Without water, everything seems bare and barren. It's a crater, a great impossible wound. How could anything withstand such hurt? Without the water, the razorfish have nowhere to hide and they lunge at the sun.

A pelican lands next to you. "It should be easier, shouldn't it? To have everything out in the open?"

The pelican begins to cry.

Mum has the candles. They're so big that when she pushes them into the cake red jam oozes out. You never thought you'd sympathise with a dessert before. You fight back the reason why.

Remember everything is ... fine.

A birth date is just another set of numbers. Sometimes you wish you were a computer that churns out ones and zeroes. Pain must be rendered inert when it's reduced to digits. It could be viewed from a distance and not be felt. What a luxury.

The cake bleeds, but Mum doesn't seem to notice. Or care.

That's not fair, is it?

Not all wounds bleed red. It's not her fault she hasn't noticed.

The door heaves open with a bang. Why wasn't it locked?

It may have been, but he has a key doesn't he? Doesn't he?

(Why!?)

"Happy birthday! Where's my favorite niece!"

Something inside withers and curls into a tight little ball in your guts. With a marionette-string wave you say, "Over here, Uncle."

A lady must always welcome her guests. Manners are the politest prisons the world thought up. Women are rarely given the key and girls are taught not to look for one.

(What you wouldn't give to voice a good, "Fuck off!")

But this isn't how the world works. Instead you raise your hand for a handshake, which he bypasses. A roadblock ignored is a death waiting for someone.

He kisses your cheek. It lingers.

It's dark.

You wake before your alarm and wonder why.

Something catches your leg. And pulls.

Ah, this is the reason. As if reason had a place in a situation like this.

You open your mouth to scream, but there's a hand already muffling it.

The cake is alight with fire, and a part of you wants it to burn the whole house down. That seems like the only logical escape. Eyes and eyes stare at you and you want to hide under your hair until it smolders.
But that's not expected of the birthday girl. You put on a happy face and endure the long minutes of 'Happy Birthday." Does anyone realise that when a smile lasts long enough, it's just baring teeth? The last 'Hurrah!' sounds and you don't look at him as you blow out your candles and wish.
Be gone.
You look up and he's still here.
You don't know what you expected. Some lingering childhood magic to still have power, maybe? Your shoulders droop. Wishes are hope's flighty foolish sister. Nothing dependable about them, they're just popped bubbles gone to soap in your palm. Better to wash them all away.
Mum smiles big and wide, clapping her hands together, "Now don't tell us your wish, or it won't come true!"
It's alright. You've gotten good at keeping secrets.

Time ticks closer to your alarm and you tense beneath your covers. You bury your head beneath the embroidered fabric and swaddle yourself with every layer you can find — the cushiest armor to ever exist. You know it will do nothing to stop him, but pretending is what children and adults do best.
You sense that you are no longer alone. That nameless prickling at the back of your neck tells you that something is in the room with you.

There's a monster inside your room. Your options are limited.
You peek an eye out and see a large lunging figure. You duck back under the covers. You would say, *there's no place like home there's no place like home*, over and over again. You would click the heels of every set of red shoes your mother owned if it would make a

difference. It's hard to wish for that when you're already here. What an impossible soapy wish.

There's mind-ending idiocy in what you do next. You brave the horrifying known and stick your neck out as eagerly as you would for the executioners' blade.

It's not what you expect.

A giant razorfish towers over you, ready to slice you open.

There's no place like home.

You heave, gasping in the mud, feeling the awful false blow of water up your nose. You feel like those fish, drowning, flopping and useless in your natural habitat —devoid of what you need most.

"I did it. Didn't I?"

The pelican doesn't answer you. Instead it looks up. Following its gaze, you notice you can no longer see the sun. The razorfish have grown so tall that they encroach on the light.

And envelop you in darkness.

Everything is … *not fine.*

The party goes on and in an artful escape you find space to breathe in the bathroom. There's something reassuring about a space designed to fit one person.

You look in the mirror, and find pink frosting smeared on the corner of your lip. You rub at it frantically. It looks redder than it should.

Mum finds you like that — cake smeared, emotion irritating your eyes and snot dripping out at an embarrassing speed. Not the happy birthday girl she was expecting. Not the girl you pretend to be.

"Honey? What's wrong?"

Even the ability to fake a smile has deserted you now. Damn it.

"It's okay, Mum. Don't worry about it."

She brushes your hands away, picks up a tissue and cleans your face. It makes you feel like a child, but for the first time today it doesn't feel like a bad thing. Being cared for used to be an unspoken gift. It's a relief to know it's still in reach.

"Now I know *it's my birthday and I'll cry if I want to* is very popular right now, but kid,' she cups your cheek, 'you don't have to take it seriously."

You laugh and it's hard to stop. Tears are coming again, faster than before. They taste so salty you want to spit them out.

"What a mess. Sorry, Mum."

"There's nothing to be sorry about, honey. It's better out than in. You don't want to dam these things up." Your mother looks at you with a gaze that grows serious without losing any of its warmth. "Are you going to tell me what's gotten you so upset?"

You shake your head. Denial taking charge so fast you're unable to do anything else. "It's nothing."

"I don't believe it is."

For a moment, you're frozen at the thought that she'll make you talk. To say the words out loud would be the equivalent of throwing a bomb into your life. It would destroy everything, leaving nothing but an empty crater behind.

"However ... since it's your birthday. I suppose I could delay the interrogation." You sag in stressed relief. "But you have to promise me that you'll do your best to make yourself happy. Most people don't know this, but you have to put in the work, to make your wishes come true."

You nod, "okay."

"That's my kid."

She leans down and drops a kiss on your forehead. In this moment you feel like things could be okay.

"If you're not feeling better soon, your uncle and I will have to cook something up to turn that frown upside down!"

With that, she dramatically sweeps out of the bathroom with a slam of the door.

Fuck.

You've decided.

You're going to drop the bomb.

You find your uncle at the jetty. Hands deep in his pockets and leaning back in his leather shoes. You think about how it wouldn't take much to tip him over. If only it was that easy.

"I'm surprised you came to find me. But not disappointed." He winks at you and it takes everything you have not to run away. Instead, you come to stop just out of his reach.

"That's enough." To your shame it comes out as a whisper.

"What was that? What does my favorite niece want?" He cocks his ear and takes a step toward you. You stumble back, desperate to keep the distance between you.

"I-I … " Deep breaths now. Do the work. "I want you gone."

"Gone? I'm your uncle, I'll always be a part of your life." He smiles, but his teeth are wrong — wide, brown and slimy. Sharp.

Fuck you.

"Fuck you!" You spit. "Go, or I'll tell."

All humor drops from his face. "What?"

"You heard me."

That's it. You've put it out there and it's taken everything you have. Bravery makes you want to throw up.

You turn and you don't even see what he slams into your head.

You wake.

And you're drowning.

Water floods your mouth and nose. A tight fist squeezes your lungs and you choke, choke, choke.

Through the murky depths and dancing seaweed you spot the most unexpected of saviors — a razorfish. It's broken in two; one piece is sharp and pointy.

It goes against your better instincts to sink deeper. To reach out when your vision is darkening and your chest burning. It only takes two of your fingertips to make contact and grip. You rise — your weapon held close to your heart.

He's lingered, waiting for the job to be done. But he's turned his back to you, like he couldn't bear to watch the final results.

His final mistake.

When it's done, his blood looks as red as the jam filling from your cake. You lean back and let the warmth of the sunbaked wooden planks dry your hair.

In the distance, you hear a shocked scream and the patter of running feet. Probably Mum. You hope she brings you another piece of cake. You feel like you could finish one now.

A pelican lands next to you and flaps its wings. It feels like a metaphor for something. You drop the bloody piece of razorfish into the water with a plonk. It's sinks deep below. Back to its home, to join your uncle.

Finally … everything really is fine.

Birthday wishes do come true.

Home Safe
Judi Morison

When the new homestead is built at Neston, Twyla is given her own room, one closed-in end of the verandah that wraps around the front and sides of the house. She's happy now she has a few hours each day away from the sharp eyes of the missus, and she can say her prayers out loud again. They sound like they have a bit more weight now and she's more confident that Jesus and His Father can hear them.

Along with her visits to the creek, she looks forward to the Sunday service. On Sundays at the mission, the Reverend used to round up any blackfellas camped nearby, make them dress in their cleanest clothes, and bring them along to the service. Sometimes men passing through or from nearby stations rode in, and then the Reverend held a proper service, with a long sermon and a lot of explaining for the blackfellas and the kids singing songs together.

But at the Neston Sunday service the missus leads them in a tuneless old hymn and the boss, red-faced and hurrying, reads a few words from the Bible and races them all through Our Lord's Prayer before they sit down to Sunday dinner. The overseer and the men, all fidgety in their cleanest clothes, come up to the house for the service too, and stay for the meal – roast beef unless the boss has been lucky enough to swap a side of his beef for an old ewe from one of the neighbours' runs.

Twyla is allowed to eat at the table on Sundays and the missus is surprised when she asks to say a prayer to bless the food. But Bella Hutchings agrees and then Twyla has a new job. Every Sunday she tries to think of different words to thank God for the food and ask his blessing on it and on them all, though she finds it hard to ask a blessing on the men, especially with George Dolphin's hard eyes fixed on her.

She can feel the strain in the men as they watch their language in front of the missus. But with the nearest neighbours twenty miles away they don't have anywhere else to go. Jack Pinnall still lets slip the odd 'Damn my soul' before his face flushes even redder when he realises what he's said. Twyla purses her lips at him then. The

Reverend was strict about swearing, especially on the Sabbath, when it's not even proper to drive a dray.

At the table, the boss and the men often talk about blackfellas. The Reverend used to call them 'our sable brethren', which sounds nearly friendly, but Tommy Parker calls them 'those black savages at our throats'. Twyla thinks it's strange that whitefellas like the Hutchings and the Neston men want to kill blackfellas when God wants to save their children. She still remembers the stories the Reverend told them about how God let His son Jesus die so that little black kids like her could be saved. But how can you be safe without your *ngambaa* and *bubaa*?

Still, Twyla looks forward to the service each Sunday. The words of the Bible readings remind her of other stories, ones she remembers hearing at a campfire with her *ngambaa*. The Reverend's big old everlasting fire still makes her feel all shivery when she thinks about it, but she loves the stories from the Bible, about how God made everything.

The book called *Genesis* tells how He made heaven and earth, all the trees and grasses, the sun and moon and stars, all the fish – even that big old one that ate that Jonah fella – and all the animals and birds. Then, after he had a big sleep on the seventh day, he made Adam and Eve. That tricky snake must have given Eve one of those little sour apples to eat because Adam and Eve got out of that garden real quick after they ate it.

Twyla likes the sound of the words from the Bible. They're something strong to hang onto, like old friends from the past, and that *Genesis* story is just like those other stories Garruu (Uncle) reminds her of, about *Baayami* and the spirit ancestors.

The seasons turn and once-strange chores are now the daily round. Calving and drafting times are hectic and the wait for the cattle cheque is always a worry for the boss. The weather is as up and down as the stock prices. Some years are wet, with the creek crossings up to the saddle flaps and Polly the only horse steady enough to try them. Other years are droughty, with the creek drying up to a string of waterholes laced together with a muddy trickle.

Twyla is never still. One or other of the Hutchings or the men always needs nursing with sunstroke or dysentery, a cold on the chest or a bump or break after falling from a horse.

After Twyla has been at Neston for four hot seasons, George Dolphin is thrown from his horse when it shies at an adder, and he's bed-ridden with a concussion of the brain. The missus has him carried up to the house and put into a bed in the boss's study. For the first week he's hardly conscious and they aren't sure he'll make it, or if the adder didn't get him as well. But the boss can't find any bite mark from the snake, nor any broken bones, so there's nothing they can do but wait and hope the bed-rest will see him clear. Now Twyla has another chore, trying to force some gruel into George Dolphin.

The man is a lot less frightening lying flat on his back in one of the boss's flouncy old nightshirts. Twyla feels sorry for him and takes her time over feeding him. Sitting on the bed beside him, she cradles his head, coaxes his lips open with the spoon, and dabs at his mouth with a corner of her pinafore when the porridge escapes his slack lips.

By the second week his eyes flutter open and she can feel his gaze burning into her as soon as she comes near his bed. He says nothing, just lies still and lets her feed him, but all the while his hard blue eyes are fixed on her face, which gets hot and prickly under his gaze, or on her chest, where her newly budding breasts are straining against the seams of her pinafore, making her face hotter still. She supports his head with just her hand now, but she still feels too closely the heat of his scalp and the throb of his blood through the mat of thick black hair that likely saved his life.

By the third week Dolphin is bolting down the gruel and muttering a few sensible words to the boss and the missus, who are relieved to see him coming good. The missus moves him from the gruel to a watery stew, which he gulps down as if making up for lost time. Twyla doesn't feed him now, just leaves the bowl and spoon with him, propping him up with a bolster so he can do for himself.

One night when she goes to collect his bowl after supper, her eyes down to escape the cold blue stare, Dolphin's hand whips out from under the sheet and grasps her wrist so tightly she squeals. Straightaway his other hand clamps over her mouth. He pulls her hand down onto the sheet between his legs and she can feel his hard *dhun* and hear his breath, heavier and faster as he rubs her claw-like hand there. As she struggles, the tin bowl falls off the bed onto the wooden floor and the metal spoon clatters across the pine planks. It creates such a racket that the missus runs in, fearing the patient has taken a turn for the worse.

Dolphin hears the approaching steps and curses Twyla. Dropping her hand, he lies back on the pillow with a sorry-sounding sigh just as the missus appears, then whines about Twyla's clumsiness, causing the missus to scold her and send her away. Twyla's happy to escape Dolphin's clutch but angry at being blamed.

She's too shamed to tell the missus what Dolphin did. She could have told her *ngambaa* but she doesn't know the proper words to say to the missus. She would just make things worse. She can't tell Garruu, either. The older man would be no match for a fully fit George Dolphin, especially if Dolphin had the other fellas to back him up, and she doesn't want to get Garruu into any more strife. Dolphin already tries to make trouble for Garruu, blaming him for any chore he or the other fellas have left undone around the homestead. And he doesn't like it one little bit when Garruu has anything to say for himself. So Twyla keeps her mouth closed and her head down and tries to avoid going near Dolphin unless the missus is around. But she still feels his eyes following her and worries what will happen when he's well enough to leave his sickbed.

Within the month Dolphin is up and about, and back on his chestnut gelding. He's even more dangerous now. He could follow her anywhere away from the homestead and no-one would be there to protect her. Twyla stays close to the house for a few days, where she can be heard if she screams – and she's made up her mind to scream loudly next time he tries anything.

On the fourth day, after she's fed the chickens, collected the eggs, watered the pumpkins and potatoes in the missus' vegetable garden and played with the station dogs' puppies, the creek calls to her. She's seen Dolphin ride out earlier with Joe Tunks, heading towards the back paddock to check on the newly-weaned calves, so she should be safe.

After a few days away from the creek the rustle of the sags is especially sweet. Twyla makes her way along the path and listens to the whispering of the tall grasses and the rattle of their ripening nuts. A memory comes of her *ngambaa* roasting corms from the sags and grinding them between stones to make into tasty cakes. Twyla's heart lifts at this new treasure she's found to tuck safely away with her few other memories.

She reaches the bank and, with a slow sigh, lets out the breath she's been holding. The creek is as she left it, quiet and busy all at once. A thunderstorm the night before has brought water purling along in the mid-morning sunlight. Ripples and eddies break up the reflections of the *gulabaa* trees bent over the water and stir up bits of weed that drift to the shallows, where a flock of *gulguwi* are picking through them. The hens rise like a small brown-grey storm cloud tinged with green, scolding her with their kak-kak cries that always make her laugh. Maybe she'll find a nest or two hidden along the bank, with some of their pale green eggs.

She squats on a satiny log at the edge of the waterhole, watching the birds settle again further up the creek, their cocky black tails and bright orange legs plain to see even from a distance. With the murmur of the water, the calls of the other *dhigaraa* along the creekline, and the chirring of *ngininnginin*, she doesn't hear the horse on the beaten earth path until it pulls up behind her.

Dolphin is off the gelding even before she springs up from the log. He takes hold of her arms and pulls her towards him so she can't run away.

'What's your hurry, girl? No need to be unfriendly.'

No use screaming. No-one will hear her. She lifts her chin.

'Leave me alone, George Dolphin. I'll tell the missus.'

'Who would she believe, eh? A filthy little gin, or me?'

Dolphin is laughing, his hands all over her. The creek is at her back and she can't push past him. She hears a seam of her pinafore tear and feels his hand on her breast, her flesh cold and shrinking even as her face burns. His other hand is up under her pinafore, poking and prodding, trying to force her legs apart as she struggles to push him away. She hears his breath quicken and sees his eyes begin to glaze. Leaning backwards slightly, she draws Dolphin forward so that he's just off-balance. Then, as he lets go of her, waving his arms around to stay upright, she steps to the side, ducks around and gives him a mighty push from behind. He takes a step forward to save himself but the edge of the bank crumbles and slides into the chuckling water, taking George Dolphin along with it.

'You black bitch!' Twyla hears as he topples.

Then he's silent, except for a few gulps and splutters as the water steals his breath, for the cold stays in the water where it's deepest. She turns to run, but then she catches a different sound. His gasps aren't just from the shock of the water. The fella's drowning. The fool can't swim.

Part of her wants to run and leave Dolphin to drown. Good riddance to him! But what would the Reverend say? She can still hear the words of those Commandments he repeated and the thought of that everlasting fire still worries her, even though she's no longer a little kid. What would her *ngambaa* say? Would she take pity on the no-good fella?

Turning back, Twyla picks up a long branch, a good arm's thickness, fallen from one of the *gulabaa* trees. Heaving it to the bank, she pushes it out into the creek towards Dolphin. His head bobs up and his bulging eyes take in her actions. With a lunge he grabs the branch and hangs on, as she stands on the other end to stop him pulling it into the waterhole. It's just enough for Dolphin to take a breath and drag himself in, arm over arm, along the silvery branch.

He reaches the bank, coughing and struggling to catch his breath. His face is grey, his clothes covered with mud and weeds. Twyla turns and catches up the loose reins of Dolphin's horse, heaves herself up on the stirrup and throws herself across the saddle. She's never ridden a horse with a saddle before; a few times she's sat astride Polly as the old mare pulled the water-sled to the creek. Now she digs her bare heels into the horse's sides like she's seen the men do and she's off along the path, leaving Dolphin to walk back. His curses follow her as she rides away but she knows he won't catch her now.

Twyla walks the horse into the dusty yard, swings her leg over the saddle and drops to the ground, still shaking from the struggle and the turn it took. She pets the gelding's coppery neck, whispers a thank-you to him for carrying her to safety, and ties the reins around the rail outside the men's hut. Then she runs across the yard, pulling her torn pinafore together at the front and combing her fingers through her wild hair.

Looking up, she sees the missus standing on the verandah. Twyla stops in the middle of the yard. Then they both watch, the missus with her hands on hips, as George Dolphin walks out from the path between the sags. His clothes are muddy, still dripping water, and he keeps his head down as he crosses the yard towards the men's hut. The missus's eyes follow him. Twyla runs up the steps and along the verandah to her room, her face burning. Then she hears Bella Hutching's voice ring out across the sun-beaten yard, much more loudly than her size would lead anyone to expect.

'George Dolphin! Lay another finger on that girl and you'll not only have me to answer to but Jack as well. Now get out of my sight and go about your proper business.'

Bella Hutchings finds Twyla on her cot, bawling now that it's all over. The missus sits beside her, patting Twyla's shoulder until her tears slow and she wipes her nose on the hem of her torn pinafore. 'Did Dolphin hurt you?'

'No missus. I pushed him in the creek but the plurry fool can't swim. I had to fish him out.'

'Good for you! He'll want to keep his distance from now on, unless he wants Mr Hutchings to show him the gate. I'll find you another pinafore – one that fits you better. And no more of that swearing, you hear?'

Twyla blows her nose again and her tears almost stop. She feels a little bit safer now, though she's shamed that the missus knows what George Dolphin tried to do. She wishes her *ngambaa* was there to talk to, to hold her and rub her back like she remembers, and make everything right.

She never speaks to Garruu of what happened but someone must have told him. A couple of days later she comes face to face with George Dolphin as he limps across the yard. He raises his head to glare at her and she sees that his right eye is bruised and swollen almost shut, and his head is cut. When she questions Garruu he grins.

'Might be that fella fall on my *bundi*.'

111

She knows she and Garruu will have to be even more careful now, but she's grateful that the other men think so little of Dolphin, or Garruu would never have gotten away with fighting a whitefella – and winning.

Glossary

Baayami	Gamilaroi creator god
bubaa	father
bundi	club
dhigaraa	bird (any)
dhun	penis
gulabaa	coolibah tree
gulguwi	black-tailed native hen
ngambaa	mother
ngininnginin	cicada

Tidal
Anne-Louise Rentell

She surfaces, gasping for air and dragging the water from her eyes with her little hands before beaming at me triumphantly.
"I did it!"
"Did what, sweetheart?" I ask.
"I was seeing how long I could stay under water without breathing", she says as she gulps. Her little chest is heaving.
Seconds before I had returned from the laundry with a clean dry towel to find her laying inert and submerged in the bath. I had frozen in horror. There were no bubbles rising to the surface of the water, just her eyes, large and staring and her dark hair a billowing seaweed halo around her head. A baby medusa.
"I could do it for a long time, mama."
I hold the towel wide as she stands up in the bath and wrap it around her tightly.
"Clever girl", I say, "but don't do it again".
"Why?"
I lift her up into my arms, and kiss her wet head.
"Because you scared me."

I close the curtains on the moon sitting low and pendulous on the watery horizon and turn to watch her small frame curled up in bed. Lit by the bedside nightlight, her face is flushed, her hair still damp around her forehead. Her eyelids, battling the descent into slumber, flicker.
Through barely parted lips she breathes:
"Where is my tail, mama?"

That night I have a dream.
I am stumbling through a lure of labyrinthine tunnels that are dark and wet. I can hear a baby crying and I am trying to reach it. Every time I think I am getting closer, the source of the cries change, the echoes ricocheting along the hard surfaces and setting me off in another direction. Soon, I am running, every now and then slipping, clawing at the dark space around me, until, in a brutal edit of the subconscious, I am at the end of a tunnel with a small wrapped and crying bundle at my feet.
The screams no longer echo, they are just the plaintive cries of a baby in distress. I reach down to pick the baby up and in that one action,

the bundle disintegrates, releasing a rush of dark water teeming with small luminescent fish.

"Mama … mama …"
A little hand is gently patting my face.
"Wake up, mama…"
Her breath on my face is sweet.
"Mama?"
I open my eyes to see her darling face peering into mine. "Get in", I say, and lift the duvet. She clambers under and I enclose her small four-year-old form in the crook of my body and the clutch of my arms.
"I love you, mama," she says.
"I love you too", I whisper into the cockle-shape of her ear.
We stay that way for a long time, before impatience gets the better of her and she wriggles free.
"Can I watch TV?" she asks.
I let her go, smiling at the normality of it, sinking into the warmth of the space she vacates and breathing it in.

When I was young, not much more than a child myself, I felt the inevitability of motherhood, understood that one day I would hold my baby in my arms postpartum, stare into her eyes, stroke her chin and in the wake of labour, feel the euphoria of love lurch in my chest. It had been preordained that I would be good at it because everyone told me so. But people can be wrong and life doesn't always turn out how we expect.

It's the first day of the school summer holidays and it is hot. The seaside promenade is busy with folk walking with casual disregard for the unwritten rule of keeping to the left. Joggers, skaters and bicyclists duck and weave through their meandering, avoiding small children running haphazardly across their paths and the sudden lunges of dogs on leash.
We hold our own against the tide, she and I, making our way in the opposite direction towards the secluded harbour. One little hand is in mine, the other is holding a bucket with a spade which rattles and scrapes as we walk. We go to the small kiosk and I order a flat white and for her the promised strawberry ice cream. After half of it ends up on the ground she removes her shoes and runs onto the beach, falling knees first into the sand, bucket and spade in tow.

I spread my towel on the concrete ledge and sit, a prime vantage point for watching her dig. I become mesmerized by her focus as she transforms small piles of sand into castle towers surrounded by moats which fill up and empty with the action of the waves.

"Is she yours?"

I turn towards the direction of a voice. There is a woman, a stranger, standing next to me, sheltering her eyes and looking out towards the water.

"Sorry?"

Taking my query as meaning I hadn't heard her, not my reticence to engage in conversation, she repeats the question.

"The little girl, is she yours?"

The sun is bright and forms a golden nimbus behind the woman, throwing her expectant shape into sharp relief.

"Yes", I say. "Yes, she is mine."

The woman nods. "She's beautiful."

We both watch silently for a moment and I don't know what else to say. Am I meant to ask her something now? How long she has to go, for instance? Does she know the sex? Will she – ?

"Well, enjoy your day."

"Thanks." I say. "You too." And as a hesitant polite afterthought, "Good luck with it all." She looks down at her hands on her belly and smiles.

"Thanks."

As she walks away, I close my eyes. Her heavily pregnant form is imprinted on the inside of my eyelids as a shape in the negative, like a figure cut from a photo. I blink the image away and turn my attention to the ants forming an orderly queue around the pooling pink ice cream on the concrete beside me. Their order, their sense of purpose both fascinates and repels me. I squash one with my finger and watch the marching unit disband in directionless confusion.

I remember my first visit to the gynaecologist, way back when. High up on the wall was a delicate sculpture of a school of silver fish. I had focused on it as the coldness of the speculum met the resistance of my cervix. The eyes of the fish averted their gaze from mine, looking instead towards the blank expanse of white wall ahead of them. I appreciated their respect for my privacy, but it was a curious choice for consultation room art. I wondered whether someone had given it to him or if he had bought it himself.

When I returned a week later to discuss my prognosis, he was kind and considerate. "You're still young enough", he said. "Let's wait and see how you respond to the medication. Let's not do anything drastic just yet."

As he wrote the script, his comb-over fell victim to gravity. I resisted the urge to reach forward and tuck the errant strands of hair behind his ear.

"Listen, mama", she says, and I don't.

It is an overcast afternoon and we are walking home along the promenade by the rock pools.

She is ten now and talking constantly. I can be forgiven for tuning out.

"Do you hear?" She grabs my hand and my attention.

"What, my love?"

She drags me to the rails overlooking the sea wall.

"The stones are singing."

I listen and she is correct. The tide is going out, the water pushing then pulling, pushing then pulling across the stony shore, playing a soft melodic sigh. She accompanies the stones in a delicate duet, her voice lifting and projecting out across the water.

The weather suddenly picks up. Her hair whips in the wind. It has grown way below her waist now and is a mane, thick and wavy like kelp. She refuses to have it cut and the hair at her nape spools itself into dreads that curl around pearls hidden from view.

I know every mother thinks their daughter special, but how many can say she wears the sea's treasures like a secret?

Before the operation, it had never really occurred to me that motherhood was something I could proactively seek. I think I thought it would just happen, if it was meant to happen. You could say I was a foolish romantic, or a fatalist.

After the operation, when the option was physically and permanently removed, I began to think differently. To think that maybe it wasn't because I was romantic or fatalistic, but simply complacent. That I hadn't formed a strong opinion about it at all, ever, preferring to "go with the flow" – whatever that means. I also thought that if I hadn't actively sought it, then perhaps I just didn't want it. Perhaps I was just pretending to myself that motherhood was something I thought I wanted. Perhaps I made a choice long ago to spite all expectations, my own included. Maybe I was thinking those things because I no longer had a choice. I don't know. Those days, I thought about it a lot.

But when I found her everything changed.

My scar twinged and pulled as I climbed over the protective railing and clambered down the rocks to the sheltered cove tucked under the lip of the cliff. It was my first swim since my recovery and I had been looking forward to the salt water on my skin and in my hair. As I tucked my swimming bag within a small cave-like opening at the cliff edge, I heard a small noise, like a cat mewing. Looking in the direction of the sound, my eyes were dazzled by sunlight darting off something shiny, nestled between the rocks. I crawled cautiously over to discover a sea-baby in earthbound form, laying on her sparkling tail like an unwrapped gift, her little arms and legs searching for purpose, her eyes screwed tight and blinking against the early dawn light.

Did someone know my business and place this beautiful foundling here for me to discover like some bizarre consolation prize? Or was it pure coincidence and her mother would collect her in due course and return with her to their fabled home beneath the waves?

I looked and I waited and I listened, holding her close, scanning the horizon. No-one came. I carefully placed the tail in my swimming bag and carried her home.

And here we are.

A wailing sound is infiltrating my dreams. At first it is low and soft – mournful, like a siren with a flat battery. But then it slowly builds in pitch and urgency until it is no longer coming from the deep recesses of my subconscious but from somewhere else entirely; her bedroom. Heart racing, I throw the bedclothes off, propel myself out of bed, crash into the door frame, stumble down the hall and slam on her bedroom light to reveal her sitting up in bed, hair wild, eyes bulging like a feral animal trapped.

"My tail! Where's my tail?!"

She's screaming, her nostrils flaring, her mouth a circle of teeth and protruding tongue.

"What have you done with my tail?!"

Her legs are sticking straight out in front of her and she's thumping them with her fists so violently they are marked bright red and white by her bashing.

"Mama's here, mama's here!". I fling myself at her and try to hold her but she resists, and her teenage strength is too much for me. Her arms break free, flailing and thrashing, her fist clipping my nose. I put my hand up to my face and my other arm out to stop her. She recoils and looks at me in shock, unsure of my response.

117

We are still, there is just the sound of our breathing now, heavy and laboured but cautious.

I taste blood in the back of my throat. I am not angry. I knew this day would come. And while I am not prepared, I know I must give in to whatever will happen next.

I gather her in my arms. "Shhhh, mama's here," I whisper, stroking her hair, kissing her forehead. Eventually she leans back, looking up at me with those beautiful pools of green.

"You're not my mother."

I throw her back on the bed like a rejected catch.

I no longer recognise her, this creature sitting across from me at the breakfast table.

She is eating fish raw, fins and all, spitting the scales across the room, scooping the eyes out with the crook of her forefinger and popping them in her mouth, sucking on them like lollies. Her hair and skin are oily and her fingers and face covered in fish guts, a string of shiny sinew dangles from her chin. It's a sight and I resist saying, "elbows off the table" and to "at least try to eat like a lady", because we're beyond this now.

Add to this that the tide was high the night before; the sea coughed up its innards and left it as a gift, like a petulant cat retching up its breakfast on the kitchen floor. Now seaweed covers the beach and smells worse than a wet bear's coat. The overwhelmingly wretched odour wafts in through the window and the smell inside is as bad as it is outside; as if the sea has entered the house and I'm drowning in a myth of my own making.

Staring at me from across the table, her eyes are like hooks.

Mustering a casual air of indifference, I ask:

"So, where did you get the fish?"

She throws her head back and laughs.

The morning she leaves, I follow her down to the beach, walking at a distance behind her as requested. Together we had managed to gently fold her tail into the confines of her school backpack. I had kept the tail a secret for the past 16 years, locked in the freezer in the garage, replenishing it with salt water as it grew from not quite a ruler's length to the size of a child's surfboard. Now her backpack is dripping, leaving a silver trail on the footpath.

Once we get to the beach, she removes all her clothes and folds them neatly on the sand. Her nakedness shimmers in the early morning light. She takes her tail from the bag and deftly slings it over her shoulder, then walks into the water.

When it is almost up to her knees, she hesitates and I think she may turn to look at me. But instead, she makes a strange movement with her right hand, a flick of her wrist. Is it a warning for me to stay away, a farewell, or simply a subconscious movement in preparation for the swim ahead? It's hard to say and at this point I am probably safe in assuming it is no longer about me.

She walks further into the water, slowly, purposefully. When it's up to her waist, she dives under, re-emerges, then takes a few confident strokes before disappearing beneath an incoming wave. Her head bobs up again and this time there is the tail which also surfaces, flicking water high in the air and catching the sunlight. She continues out further now with speed, not looking back once until she is barely visible, then not visible at all.

I move down the beach to where her bag sits stranded and I wait, just in case. I wait there all day as the tide goes out, the shadows lengthen and the air grows cold. The sun makes one final caress of the horizon, like a parting lover's hand on the cheek of her beloved, and dips behind the escarpment.

Tightrope
Emma Ashmere

Tightrope
Roll up, roll up,
Come see the Female Blondin
Will she walk across the Thames
Or will she fall to drownin'?

All morning half of London had been swarming past the house.
Father directed me to shut the window against 'the rabble'. I did as
he said. I'd been listening for the doorbell, you see. Tilly was going
to send a message, and I'd excuse myself from the breakfast table.
There it was now. I set down my spoon, and said, 'No Father, I will
go.'
There was nobody at the door, only a green leaf folded into the
shape of a star left on the step. I picked it up, inhaled the summer
green, and almost wept. I'd rehearsed the next moments so many
times: throwing on my oldest coat, tiptoeing towards the cupboard
under the stairs, taking up my carpetbag, checking its contents: my
sketching book, charcoals, phials of pigment, brushes; bread, apples
and cheese; and various other necessities.
'Who is it?' Mother called down.
I ran down the steps out into the fray, picking my way over the
muddy wheel ruts and wooden pavement planks, jostling with the
raggedy shawls and dusty skirts, melting in with the crowds
funneling down to the river.
When I reached the chandlers shop, I dared to stop and look back for
Tilly.
'I'll wear my new red hat,' she'd said. 'And you'll wear yours.'
'No, I'll wear the old brown one.'
'I see. Camouflage.'
Still no sign of her. Good. I rushed past the sailors lounging in their
pea coats, the young girls selling lavender, and the so-called
Crawlers, as my parents persisted in calling them, rattling their
begging bowls.
Onwards towards Battersea Bridge. There was Raff, the chandlers
lad, perched up high, clinging to a pole above the fray.
I pushed my way through the wall of flesh, ignoring the curses and
elbows.
Easy does it, Mrs.
We got here first.

'Let her pass,' Raff was saying. 'I'm saving the lady painter her place. She was here at first light.'

I blinked at his lie, and reached the railing of the bridge relatively intact. As I offered the spy-glass up to Raff I noticed the scars and burns of his hands from the candle-making. These same hands ran midnight letters between Tilly and me. What was that, if not a lie? The heat of unwashed bodies pressed all around. I wiped the sweat from my eyes, and squinted up at the tightrope, slung far higher than the bridge, cutting the usual view in half. The brown-grey sky above, the brown-green river below bristling with watercraft.

I managed to extricate my sketching book and move a stub of charcoal across the page, the other passion my parents forbade. The trick was to capture the main elements of any scene, big or small, without too much thought. I blocked out the scores of wherries, steamers, and barges crammed with gaping spectators. All were sitting low in the murky currents, creaking at their mossy anchor chains.

My arm was shoved, causing the charcoal to skid across the page. I smudged any erratic lines, and continued on.

A band played somewhere. Barrow boys cried out. *Oy-sters, oy-sters, penny a parn! Roll up, roll up.*

Roll up for the beginning or the end. I glanced around for Tilly's red hat. She'd worn it at her first drawing lesson.

'Focus on the points of interest, you say, Miss Ada?' That's what she'd said as she gazed at me.

We'd been introduced at one of the bluestocking soirees my parents had forbidden me to attend. I'd pretended I was going to church, but I'd met Tilly in Hyde Park beneath the nodding trees. We watched the po-faced nannies wheeling screaming babes, catching snippets of conversations between bored husbands and unhappy wives.

'Yes,' I'd said, trying to maintain the air of a professional drawing instructor. 'Concentrate on the essential elements of form.'

Tilly laughed.

'What's so funny?' I'd said.

'The only points of interest in Hyde Park are your eyes.' She took my hand and squeezed it.

I held up my charcoal as a measuring stick, estimating the proportions of the five small barges positioned at equal points across the span of the river beneath the waiting high wire. This sketch had to be good, good enough to sell to Tilly's friend at the newspaper. I could almost feel her peering over my shoulder. *This angle here, Ada. Too blunt. And what about the barges.*

I turned my attention to the barges' masts, tethered to the tightrope by a system of guiding ropes, presumably to keep it in firmly in place while the Female Blondin walked her rope, defying the doubters, doomsayers, scoffers and scorners.

Her starting place would be the Battersea wharf. Her destination, the site of the old Cremorne Pleasure Gardens, that sooted clump of greenery on the Chelsea side, where fortune tellers and exotic musicians once beguiled the restless London rich.

I searched the greys and browns of the banks for a splash of red. There, over there on the Battersea banks, a flourish of scarlet. But it was not Tilly. It was the star of today's spectacle – Miss Selina Young – for that was The Female Blondin's real name.

Posters had been plastered over windows and walls for weeks. Tilly and I studied them all. In one version Selina Young was mannish, thick-necked, sturdy-legged, with the forehead of a bison. In another she was dew-eyed, terrified, as frail and flighty as a hummingbird. Somebody had christened her the Female Blondin. Tilly thought it a compliment comparing her to the famous high-wire walker Monsieur Charles Blondin. I suspected it was an attempt at insult and belittlement. A way to say surely a maiden could never achieve the glories of the great Blondin, bedazzling all at The Great Exhibition, or bowling along blindfolded backwards over the roar of Niagra Falls.

'She's one of us, don't you think?' Tilly had said.

We both agreed, yes, whatever the direction of Selina Young's intimate passions, she was one of us in her determination, strength, and refusal to conform to a future not of her own making.

All heads turned to watch as Selina Young appeared, surrounded by a knot of people moving along the Battersea banks towards a makeshift wooden tower. She ran up the tower, her green cape fluttering after her. A man joined her at the platform, and raised a handkerchief to test the force and fickleness of the wind.

I tucked my book under my arm, and asked Raff for the spy-glass. Down the tunnel of refracted prisms of mirror and brass, the bright medallion of Selina Young's face. She was nothing like the posters. Her high cheekbones were licked with rogue, the strong chin resolute, her eyes fulsome, serious. With the grace of a dancer, she swished off her cape and cast it aside. Her skirts jutted out stiff and short, revealing her white-stockinged legs, which seemed sculpted from marble, rather than bone and flesh.

Her dark smooth hair flowed loose beneath a cap as she gazed around. The man behind her said something. The red kerchief dropped.

A great roar rose up.

In the boats below, every face was held skywards. Some outstretched their arms, as if ready to catch her should she fall. A clutch of paddle-boats waited by the wharf. The only movement, puffs of smoke wisping from the stacks, and a lurch as people rushed to one side for a closer look.

Silence fell as Selina Young took up a long balancing pole and paddled it in her hands, as if weighing it, perhaps even blessing it. She stood very still, took a breath.

One slipper inched out in front of the other until she was out from safety the platform and standing over the water.

The sun flung out a celebratory ray. For a moment, the tightrope vanished in the glare, absorbed into the haze and smoke. She appeared to tread unsupported through the air. A flock of swallows rose up and swooped around her, welcoming her into their realm.

I stared at her until the white of her legs turned dark and left a shimmering imprint on my eyes, until it was only the two of us, she and I, the watcher and the watched, linked together by an invisible thread of...

I was shoved forward against the rail so hard I almost dropped the spy-glass. By the time I looked up again, Selina Young had come to a wavering halt.

One foot was on the rope. The other was raised in the air.

What's she doing? somebody said.

It's part of the act.

Everyone agreed. It was part of the act – until she sat down on the rope. Her legs dangled either side from the huddle of red-green skirts. One hand clutched the balancing pole. Her head did not move, her eyes still trained on the other side of the bank.

Slowly she raised herself. One foot slid forwards. Then the other. Onwards she crept towards the fourth barge. But the tightrope had begun to slouch lower beneath every step. The Cremorne Gardens lay only fifty yards away but it may as well have been fifty miles.

A collective gasp rose up as the balancing pole slithered from her hands and hit the water with a slap. The tightrope cavorted beneath her, backwards and forwards like a garden swing. She sat down, and clung on.

Roll up, roll up.

She's for it now.
A slip of a girl, daring to defy gravity.
Female Blondin is falling down, falling down, my sweet lady.
A scuffle broke out on the Chelsea banks. A ripple of panic sped through the crowds. People shouted. Others screamed. Wagers were laid on whether she'd plummet, and if she did, if she'd live.
Above, Raff was calling out to someone.
'What is it?' I handed up the spy-glass.
'The guy ropes, Miss. They're saying they've been cut from the mast of the fourth barge.'
An accident?
A chill wind cut the water, riffling boats, as if the ancient deities of the Thames had tired of the day's interlopers, and now conspired to drive us off.
Sabotage.
I kept my eyes on her as the rope continued to sway, and promised to hold a vigil for her until the end, whatever that end proved to be, hoping the strength of my gaze would save our intrepid acrobat from slipping down into ignominy and calamity, and rescue her as surely as any ladder, mast, or rope.
I was concentrating so hard on my task I barely heard Raff shout, 'Look, Miss.'
A boat had manoeuvred its mast beneath the rope. Slowly, calmly, Selina Young climbed down.
I didn't move from my place until she'd been ferried safely to the bank, where she was hurried away wrapped in a coat. The crowds had begun to dribble away. I stared at the water, at the bits of paper and rubbish bobbing there.
Tilly has not come.
Raff was calling to me.
No, it wasn't Raff. It was Tilly.
'Ada?'

Here she is, Tilly, taking my arm, whispering how she loves me, how I must never doubt her, that she was trapped on the other side of the bridge and tried to call out to me. Now she's kissing my cheek, and my mouth, here in the fading light, offering to carry my bag, telling me to hurry to catch our train.

Do you remember, Tilly, what the newspapers said: *A heroic failure. A brilliant Miss! We adore the Female Blondin all the more for her spectacular Miss-step!*

Remember my illustration, how we laughed and cried to see it so finely engraved by your friend at the newspaper, how they published it under my new name. A. Greenleaf.

And the advertisements we put in. *Miss Greenleaf, Portrait Painter & Artistic Instructor of Distinction.*

My head was still so full of visions of her, of you, I didn't care what might befall us that first night of our escape. You found that tiny room over the haberdasher's shop in Brighton, the sea wind battering at our door. Remember how you carried in an easel you'd made for me balanced on your shoulder and set it by the grey window light and said, 'Welcome home, Ada, my love.'

While I waited for my first drawing students to flock to our studio, I compiled all those clippings from newspapers about Selina Young. Pictures of her with flowers in her hair. Or wearing a cap. Wearing pantaloons beneath short skirts. In a dress so long it covered her feet. Large eyes, small nose. Vice versa. Marching along her rope. Paralysed, inert. Unruffled by the clamour as she strode along, never looking down at the flotilla below.

And the mocking captions beneath those illustrations.

Death On The Rope

Madam Blondin all amuses, as a bridge a rope she uses.

If she had fallen into the river, she would have found it soft.

'I'll invite her to sit for me, Tilly,' I said. 'I'll paint her portrait for no fee. That will pique the public's interest more than any advertisement.'

We talked about it in great detail, between me visiting parlours, tea rooms, concerts and soirees touting for paying sitters, and Tilly working all hours below in haberdashery shop, both of us pretending we weren't hungry or cold, or gnawed by fear and regret. We imagined Selina Young here, watching me while I set out my brushes. Her manner would be easy. Her eyes intelligent. Her accent, born from the north country, or the street. She wanted to appear as herself, she said. No showy costumes. Just as herself, seated straight-backed in a simple upright chair, not dangling from ropes, or spinning upside down from the ceiling. No swallowing swords or breathing flames or being shot out of a canon in a wreath of smoke, or whatever else her daredevil family had trained her up to make a crust.

And so when the mesmerizing Selina Young agrees to visit our rooms, I'll have already rehearsed my lines. We'll discuss the scale, content, atmosphere and vision of the portrait required. I'll take up the crayon and stare at my luminous sitter, searching for what is hidden, listening for what is unsaid, working to conjure the balance of serenity and energy, courage and caution, shining in her eyes. After an hour, Selina Young takes my hand in her cool marble grasp, and says, 'I must go, Miss Ada. There's another ravine to skip across.'
Her grip is so strong it will anchor me to the new life Tilly and I've dreamt up.

And when she's gone, Tilly, you'll lie on your back on our bed and study my attempts and say Selina Young looks both younger and older than we ever were or will ever be.
'Why?'
'Because she's already glimpsed infinity.'

At the end of her second sitting she'll ask us both to join her in the travelling burlesque performer's life. We'll thank her and politely decline, and watch from the window as she swaggers away down the sea-fogged esplanade, one hand waving above her hat because she knows we will be watching her all the way.
The following week, a small article will appear in the newspaper, reporting that The Female Blondin, Miss Selina Young, has tried again to walk over the Thames again. No fanfare, no posters, no street-singers. She walks it there and back successfully, five times.
'To think she didn't tell us,' Tilly says.
'Just goes to show,' I say. 'The portrait painter never sees all.'

The following year, another article: *Dressed in a suit of armour, while wheeling a barrow loaded with fireworks across a rope one hundred feel aloft when...*
'Stop, Tilly. I cannot hear it.'

Some days later we learn Selina Young is not dead. She's confined to a chair.

I decide to write to her, and ask if I might paint her portrait again. We'll go to her cottage, and take a basket of bread, apples, cheese and wine, because we know how it is to feel hunger's bite. We'll talk of the world and she'll still be the most perfect sitter, poised but not posed, open but not shallow.

We'll return several times to her cramped little lodging room, and bring her finished portrait hidden beneath a tasselled cloth Tilly has borrowed from the haberdasher shop. Tilly will throw it off with a magician's flourish.

After Selina has told us how much she admires the portrait, we'll take her hand and see if she can clasp a paintbrush or a crayon between her fingers. We'll smile as she loops it across the page, creating mountains, rivers, seas, flames, birds, the fluttering flags of circus tents.

'You are a woman of rare perspective,' Tilly will say.

She'll raise her eyes to us. And we'll both nod.

But I never did write that letter, did I, Tilly. I never did paint her sitting straight-backed in a chair in our damp little salt-bitten room above a shop.

I was too busy. Word had spread of my abilities with the brush. All manner of sitters lined up at my door. Paintings by A. Greenleaf hang on the walls of Brighton, and beyond.

Show me the illustration again, Tilly, the one from the newspaper, signed for the first time with my show-name: A. Greenleaf all those years ago.

Everyone has forgotten us now. My parents have long since stopped putting those advertisements in the newspapers to seek me out.

Remember that Greek poetess of antiquity who said: *someday, somewhere, someone will remember us.*

I'm not sure that's true.

Look at us here, sitting in the warm, sipping wine, two blurred greying figures ensconced behind the window glass, forgetting nothing, holding hands, watching the horizon line slung like a rope above the waves.

Waiting
Sikwasa Van Zutphen

The tired remains that lay on my bathroom floor are now unrecognisable. My skin has lost its shape—its life—and droops heavily around the perimeter of my frame like a candle melted in a heat wave. Once sun-kissed and soft, it is now a deep brown, and stiff like old leather. My new yellow house dress is a canvas to ghastly fluids that have soaked and dyed it a deep, dirty green. The body that I spent so much time and energy and money to render attractive taunts me with an insistence that it was a pointless endeavour; that I, like everyone, was just another clumsily assembled tower of meat and bones barely held together by an ageing wall.

Death, I have learned, very rapidly collapses the tower. It pulls its foundations from beneath it, and lets it fall heavily where gravity commands, knees upon tiles, breasts upon tiles, forehead upon tiles with a thwack. My body still lies in the position that he left it in, legs crossed at the ankles, the skirt of my dress hitched up onto my back. Where did he go when he left me, when it was over? He fled from the bathroom, yes, but did he run away, as far as he could, as if distance would erase what he had done? Or did he linger, numb and unsteady and unbelieving? After the screaming and the struggle, after he did what he had long promised he would do, the final sound my body heard was the sharp ringing of yet another frequency dying. Did he, too, hear the ringing in his ears? At that moment when his fist made contact with the back of my head, when his rage burst from his body and hit mine with a dull eggshell crack, did something pass between us, a final shared experience between husband and wife? Twenty-seven days later, does he still hear the ringing? And if he does, how is he trying to silence it? Booze? The races? Or company loud and uncivilised enough to give him something else to worry about?

When I first became aware of my predicament, the separation of my consciousness from my body, the ringing was still in my ears, and I was sure he was still in the house, somewhere. I thought I heard him in our bedroom, rifling through my hat boxes, opening the drawers of my dresser one by one. I thought I heard the chimes of my jewellery box ballerina dancing before being snuffed out with a thud. I thought I heard him in the kitchen, too, the jingling of glass bottles in the refrigerator as he opened it with too much force, the sound of him slamming the bottle top off a beer using the edge of the kitchen table for leverage. And when I thought I heard these sounds, pushing through the ringing in my ears, I wondered how long he would stay. I wondered whether he would still come in to use the bathroom when he had drunk just enough, stepping over the hurdle in his way. I was dead, of course, but even in death, I feared what version of him would come lurching through the door, and braced for what version of me I would need to become. I waited for hours, taunted by the uncertainty of whether he would come in, and then by my own uncertainty of myself. Could I really hear him? Was he really there? Or were the sounds a figment of my imagination, a pastiche of experiences that still lingered in my subconscious? And had I brought them into being because it felt more natural to wait in fear? Four weeks later, I don't know whether it was Ted or my mind inhabiting our house, but as the sun started to set on that first night, the sounds of his presence faded along with the ringing in my ears and the carmine glow of the setting sun.

And for the first time in twenty-five years, my fear of him faded too.

The next morning, I began waiting to be found and one fear was quickly replaced by another. As I watched my skin turn blue and purple and distend, my lips expand and my tongue swell, I imagined who might find me and what they might think. I worried who would walk in to see my dress up over my back, my exposed panties now stained with the contents of my bowel and bladder. I worried that they would stop seeing me as an object of admiration and see me, instead, as an ageing, incontinent woman: something to be ignored, overlooked, a blemish. I worried that they might gossip and reach conclusions, and that they would rewrite their recollections of me. That I would cease to be Mrs Ted Thompson, respected member of the Horsham Ladies' Association, and instead become the object of pity and judgement. Had I brought this on myself? Most likely. Ted is a respected man - the manager of the local bank. When people are down on their luck, Ted is their salvation. When people need money to fund their dreams, Ted is their golden goose. What's more, Ted is handsome. Solid build, tanned skin, creases folded with years of great responsibility, thick hair streaked with wisdom. For Ted to have done what he did, if he did, I must have done something atrocious to provoke him. Had I had an affair? Bankrupted us with too much shopping? Gotten too drunk and taken his gun out of storage? I was always drinking, they will say, always fixing guests a sweet vermouth as an excuse to have yet another myself. And it was getting earlier and earlier in the day, too. I was probably having them with my morning cup of coffee. Imagine what Ted would have had to come home to, at the end of a hard day at work? Imagine the state I must have been in on a daily basis. It's almost unbelievable.

129

The fact is, I worried that they might say these things because I knew that I would too.

During that time, as I daydreamed my way through the many responses that my death might trigger, I tried to find a way to fix myself up, to bring my petticoat, the skirt of my dress, back down over my thighs. To claw back at least some reason for the Ted that they knew to have wanted to stay with me. To refasten the lock of hair that had come loose in the struggle, to make myself look as I always made sure I did look - perfect. But as soon as I tried, I realised I couldn't. My fingers made contact with my dress, with my hair, but it was as if I had been sitting on them. I could see them clearly, could wriggle them, but I couldn't feel nor pick up a thing. I had lost my ability to touch.

After five days, I realised, slowly and then suddenly, that the isolation that I was experiencing in death merely echoed the isolation that I had felt in life. Not always, of course. Not as a child, playing on the farm and raising my poddy lambs. Not as a young teenager, attending Girl Guides with Betty and Shirley and Barb. Not as an eighteen-year old, when a handsome clerk took me out to the pictures and to dinner and to meet his family and said that he was sure he had met the girl for him. Not as a nineteen-year-old bride, the envy of Betty and Shirley and Barb, attending important society events in clothes from the department store in the city as Mrs Ted Thompson. But by twenty, when the honeymoon was over, Ted's days at the bank grew longer and longer and a chill set in. By twenty-two, Betty and Shirley and Barb had moved to the city themselves, and I was in my big empty house counting the days on my calendar as Dr Brown had instructed. Ted said I hadn't let him down, that I was still the most good-looking girl in the town, a real catch. I knew that he was lying, but I told myself he wasn't. I didn't want to risk probing him on it, either. I didn't want him, or me, to realise the truth.

As his position at the bank grew in importance, he was called away on more business trips, and I began to find other things to keep me company: drinking, gossiping, shopping. I joined the Horsham Ladies' Association, and made new friends, the wives of other important men, men like Ted. Was I isolated then? At the time I couldn't put my finger on why, but an emptiness had begun to grow inside of me that I would, in time, realise I didn't know how to fill. I was present, yes, often surrounded by important people pulsing with the rhythm of life, and yet I was, somehow, always alone.

And so, twenty-eight years into my marriage, twenty-five years into the acceptance of my barren state, twenty-four years into assuming a front of faultless desirability, it was no wonder that I, at my most vulnerable and real, hadn't been found. No-one knew to be looking. I was waiting for a rescue party that didn't know I needed rescuing because I had been too ashamed to signal for help. But wasn't I right to do what I did and keep to myself?

Weren't there a set of razor-sharp nails on each one of my friends ready to rip me to shreds, to dismantle my foundations, at the slightest sign of weakness? Yes, of course, they thrived on weakness: weakness was power, ammunition. We weren't friends, not really, because as we talked and shopped and celebrated and campaigned, we were always keeping a keen eye towards the floor, hoping that something terrible would emerge from the depths of our pasts to drag someone down and devour them.

I watched my discoloured corpse begin to dissolve in an eruption of gasses and liquids, and what I could only imagine was the putrid smell of my flesh disconnecting from my bones and spoiling. By that stage, day ten, I had lost my sense of smell, and while I was saved the horror of smelling my own body rot and fester, it became clear that the self that had accompanied me throughout my time on earth had been slipping away from me long before my murder. I was, in life, it seemed, a terrible person. I wasn't always, but for the most part, I was. And, perhaps as some eternal punishment, my death didn't bring me peace. While my body decomposed day after day, I was forced to watch my true nature seethe to the surface and spoil my polished exterior, deteriorate my facade. While at first I had dreaded being found, I now wondered if I ever would. Was being forgotten the price I would have to pay to maintain my faultless image? Was it better to remain a beautiful picture, even if that picture was a forgery?

It was around day 22 that my vision started to fade. I realised as I sat atop the toilet cistern, looking out the window. At first I thought that I had been staring into the sunlight for too long, as over the last few days, I had begun to once again find beauty in the small things, the natural things, beyond my house's walls. The dew on the grass, on the webs spun by golden orb spiders, first thing in the morning. The way the yellow leaves on the full moon maple didn't just fall, but jolted then teetered then wafted their way down to the gravel driveway. The patchwork quilt of the multicoloured crab apple. As it faded, my vision danced with dust fairies and stars. I covered my eyes with my hands to reset them, and when I re-opened them, the garden had become a watercolour smudge, the bathtub a blurry white cloud, my corpse a still brown pool.

When there was nothing else left, over the last five days, my ears took control of my whole being, pulling me from one sensation to the next. A thunderstorm: at first a dull rumble, getting louder, then a loud crack of lightning. Water hitting the roof, rolling into the gutters, pouring down the drain. And then, the birds chirruping as the water stopped and the land dried, the creak of shifting temperatures expanding and detracting the floorboards of the house, the buzz of a hive of bees working in the day and retiring at night, working then retiring, working then retiring.

On my last day, I heard a noise I hadn't heard in days, weeks, years? Children, two children— boys—approaching the tennis court next door. Our neighbours' kids home from boarding school for the long weekend. At first, they didn't say anything I could decipher— they were too far away. But I could hear from the steady whoomping of the tennis ball that their game had improved a great deal since last Summer. The "out", too, was called equally by each of them, suggesting they were evenly matched. They played a good, quick game. The eldest won, but was a good sport. He called for another game, and the youngest agreed. It was his serve. But then, a whoomp, different to the others. And, a crash through glass close by. Footsteps crunching on gravel - our gravel, the gravel on our driveway. A knock on the door—our door.

"Excuse me?"

Another knock.

"I don't think they're home…Wait, what's that? Can you smell that?"

"Disgusting."

"I'm going to get Dad."

Footsteps crunching the gravel again, fast, eager. Then, minutes later, the lighter footsteps, still fast, joined by heavier, steadier footsteps. The footsteps of Frank, our neighbour, Ted's friend.

"Can you smell that, Dad?"

Another knock, heavier.

"Kate? Kate, are you in?"

Another knock, heavier, faster.

"Step back, boys."

The sound of the door being rammed. Once, twice and he was in.

"It's worse in here."

"Boys, go to the house, and ask your mother to call Sergeant White. Go on now, quick."

Light footsteps running on gravel, while heavier footsteps thudded on floorboards.

Closer. Closer. Turning the bathroom doorknob with a soft creak.

"Oh Christ."

The door closed once again, and Frank's heavy footsteps thudded back through the house, to the kitchen. The feet of the linoleum chair scraped on the floor as he pulled it out and sat at the kitchen table. Though he was all the way in the kitchen, several rooms distant, I could hear him sigh. And then he breathed, wresting control of his lungs.

In and out.

In and out.

Before the third breath, the sound faded, crackled, muffled, muted, stopped.

The wait was over.

Author Bios

Eunice Andrada is a poet, educator, and organizer. Her debut poetry collection "Flood Damages" (Giramondo Publishing, 2018) won the Anne Elder Award and was a finalist for the Victorian Premier's Literary Award for Poetry and the Dame Mary Gilmore Award. She has performed her poetry on diverse international stages, including the UN Climate Conference in Paris, Sydney Opera House, and Parliament of New South Wales. Her previous work has been awarded the John Marsden & Hachette Australia Prize (2014) and been shortlisted for the Fair Australia Prize (2018). Her poetry is currently featured in the Museum of Sydney, as part of the exhibition "A Thousand Words". She serves as a judge for the Kenneth Slessor Poetry Prize in the 2020 New South Wales Premier's Literary Awards.

Emma Ashmere writes long and short fiction. Her critically acclaimed debut novel, The Floating Garden, was shortlisted for the 2016 Small Press Network MUBA prize. Her short stories have been widely published, and shortlisted for the 2019 Commonwealth Writers Short Story Award, 2019 Newcastle Short Story Award, 2018 Overland NUW Fair Australia Prize, and the 2001 Age Short Story Competition. She has a PhD in marginalised histories from La Trobe University, a MA from the University of Adelaide, and is a recipient of the QWC/Olvar Wood mentorship for LGBTQIA+ writers. Her new short story collection Dreams They Forgot is published by Wakefield Press.

Rebecca Dale is a writer and librarian, obsessed with all things in the dark waiting to be discovered. She lives in Sydney with two partners and a recalcitrant rabbit.

Brenna Gautam is a lover of literary fiction currently residing in Washington D.C. with her cat Pip. She has previously published one short story with Baby Teeth Journal and one poem with Tuck Magazine, in addition to several nonfiction articles on national security topics written during her time in law school. She likes to write about women's issues, outer space, and revolutions against unjust systems, and she's currently working on a novel touching on these themes.

Maeve Henry lives in Oxford, England, and writes poetry and fiction. Her poetry has been widely published, most recently in Presence, The Alchemist's Spoon and Ink, Sweat and Tears. She was shortlisted for the Brotherton Prize in 2019 and the Wasafiri Prize in 2018. She holds a Masters in Creative Writing from Oxford Brookes University, and works in hospital administration.

Isabella Luna is a queer writer and performing artist living and working on Dharawal, Wodi Wodi, and Eora lands in NSW, Australia. She holds a BCA (Hons) in Writing at the University of Wollongong. Her work has been featured in various publications and festivals, including: Cordite Poetry Review; the Wollongong Writers Festival; Baby Teeth Journal; Sydney's Story-Fest; and once in Texas via Skype. Find her on Twitter: @bellalunapoet

Fiona Lynch is a Melbourne-based writer. Her work has been published in Cordite Poetry Review (2020), as a prize winner in the Grieve Poetry Prize (2020) and she was shortlisted in the ACU Prize for Poetry (2018 & 2020). Her poetry was highly commended in the W. B. Yeats Poetry Prize for Australia (2019). Fiona's illustrated poem 'The Star and the Tsar' was shortlisted in the Fair Australia Prize (2019) and she was shortlisted in the Newcastle Poetry Prize (2017). Fiona's poetry is published in several Australian anthologies and also in Ireland. Fiona has written television comedy and worked as a stand-up comedian at iconically seedy venues in Melbourne.

KJ Mair is currently an emerging writer. She has studied screenwriting at the Australian, Film Television & Radio School (AFTRS) for two years. She has won second prize in both the Alice Sinclair Memorial Prize (2016) and the Newcastle Herald Short Story completion (2019). She has also been a finalist in numerous writing competitions, has had stories published in the Newcastle Herald and the Hunter Professional Arts Magazine and has been shortlisted for the Drowned Earth (2019) anthology. In 2020 she was an editor and contributor to her writer's group (Lake Macquarie Branch of the Fellowship of Australian Writers) anthology, Beneath the Surface.

Dasha Maiorova is a Belarus-born writer who lives and works on Dharawal Country in Sydney's south. Her writing has been published in The Big Issue, Voiceworks and Baby Teeth. She is currently working on her first manuscript, a contemporary literary gothic set in Saint Petersburg, which was long-listed for the Richell Prize. She has recently fallen in love with aerial lyra, and dreams of combining this physical art form with writing and painting. She writes about books and reading at www.dashamaiorova.com

Four female-identifying artists met at a poetry slam in Wollongong. Moved by each other's unique voices and united in their love of words, they created Medusa's Daughter: a place to share their furies and vulnerabilities through performance. A study in riot and rhythm, joy and sorrow, rage, power, hope and forgiveness, **Medusa's Daughter** aspires to strike dissonant harmonies that explore the multifaceted nature of womanhood. They can't promise their words won't encourage revolution, but they can promise not to turn anyone into stone.

Judi Morison is of Gamilaroi and Celtic heritage and lives in the Illawarra, where she writes short fiction, creative non-fiction and poetry, and is working on a second novel while waiting for a publisher to snap up her first. Judi is editorial assistant for Dreaming Inside: Voices from Junee Correctional Centre, an annual anthology of writing by Aboriginal inmates, and is currently completing a Master of Arts in Creative Writing at UTS. Judi's work includes 'The Plain' (Red Room Poetry, 2014), 'Coast Line Dreaming' (2019 UTS Writers' Anthology), 'If' (TEXT Journal Special Issue No. 58: The in/completeness of human experience, 2020), 'Bone Dry' (2020 UTS Writers Anthology) and 'Sean' (2020 ACE Anthology).

Raksha Muthukumar is a technologist, activist, and storyteller; she's a coder at Google by day and spends the rest of her time fighting for progress. You can find Raksha at a protest, in a beer garden, or online at www.raxsha.me

Lieu-Chi Nguyen is a Vietnamese-Australian emerging writer born in Sydney and residing in Far North Queensland. She is a member of Sweatshop: Western Sydney Literacy Movement and has been published in SBS Voices, Sweatshop Women Volumes One and Two and this little red thing. Lieu-Chi grew up in a culture with an oral storytelling tradition and wanted to capture these memories, as well as explore mother-daughter relationships in The Long Boobed Ghost (first published in Sweatshop Women).

Jaya Penelope is a storyteller and poet whose work traces the feathery footprints of the beloved from kitchen sink to fairytale forest and back again.

Louise Pieper is a lawyer, a librarian and a lexophile. She's been told she's too smart for her own good, wears too much black, has too many books and reads too much, but she doesn't believe any of those things is possible. She does believe that stories can change the world; hers have been published in volumes one and two of the Heroines Anthology and A Hand of Knaves and the soon to be released Unnatural Order (CSFG Publishing, 2018 and 2020). She writes about writing and shares stories at www.louisepieper.com.

Marija Poljak is a high school teacher and writer of fiction who lives in Adelaide, South Australia. She teaches English, Women's Studies and Aboriginal Studies and is passionate about social justice. Marija's writing focuses on the experiences of girls and women and explores themes of identity, belonging, love and change. Her writing is largely inspired by her Slavic background and the people, events, stories and myths of the Balkan region. Her debut novel is The Courtyard Children.

Anne-Louise Rentell is a theatre-maker with more than 20 years experience as a director, performer, dramaturg and writer. As an independent artist, she is committed to creating female-centred stories and has written and performed her own works "The Governess in Lessons Learnt" and "One Rotten Apple". She is currently working on "The Siren Project", a new music theatre work comprised of six poetic monologues sung by six women, based on oral histories gathered from residents of Port Kembla, NSW. While living in London, she wrote for Total Theatre Magazine and co-authored "Abstract Vaudeville: The Work of Rose English", a monograph of UK performance artist Rose English. Recently, she has been enjoying expanding her storytelling to short fiction and screenplays.

Beth Spencer's books include Vagabondage (UWAP 2014), How to Conceive of a Girl (Random House 1996) and The Party of Life (Flying Islands, 2015). She has won a number of awards, including the Carmel Bird Digital Award for The Age of Fibs, and lives and writes on Darkinjung land on the Central Coast, NSW. www.bethspencer.com

Rita Tognini is a Western Australian writer of poetry and short fiction. She has worked as a teacher and public servant. Among the themes she likes to explore are the relationship of language, landscape and identity across continents, the intersection of the personal and the political and the complexity of relationships and family ties. Her work has won prizes and commendations and has been published in a wide range of collections and journals. In 2018, Rita was selected for the Four Centres Emerging Writer Program and is currently working on short fiction and poetry collections.

Sikwasa Van Zutphen is a writer, editor, and teacher. She is a mid-to-high-functioning introvert whose writing voices the experiences of the silenced, marginalised, and socially awkward. In her spare time, she continues to write short fiction while also working towards a novel. She studied Literature, as well as Writing, Editing, and Publishing at UQ, and lives with her family in Brisbane.

Romy Tara Wenzel is a writer and artist in Melukerdee country, Tasmania, exploring mythology and ecology through an animist perspective. 'Yama Uba' is from her short story collection, 'Gorgon', that seeks to compassionately re-voice female antagonists in folk tales.

Anthea Yang is a writer whose work has appeared in publications such as Djed Press, Hypertrophic Literary and Underground Writers. She has performed at Spoken Word Perth and Melbourne Writers Festival, and her poetry was shortlisted for the Dorothy Porter Award for Poetry in 2020.

A.B. Young is a queer-identifying, witchcraft-practicing, dual-passport-holding purveyor of the uncanny in the mediums of fiction, collage, and zine. This is her second fiction publication. Her first, a short story called 'Vain Beasts', was published in Lady Churchill's Rosebud Wristlet and won the 2019 PEN America/Robert J. Dau Short Story Prize for Emerging Writers.

Nicky Zhang is a Chinese-New Zealander living in Melbourne. She studied law and philosophy at the University of Canterbury, and works in finance. Nicky has a keen interest in ancient Greek history and mythology; she previously appeared on the BBC's "Mastermind" programme with Alexander the Great as her specialist subject.

Sarah Nicholson is the creative director of The Heroines Festival and editor of the Heroines Anthology. She is an academic and writer who teaches in literature, philosophy, creative arts, gender and religious studies. She is a past director of the National Young Writers' Festival, awardee of the Ian Potter Cultural Trust for Literature, and recipient of a Writer's and Translator's Centre of Rhodes fellowship. She was the 2017 Emerging Writer in Residence for the Katherine Susannah Pritchard Writers' Centre. She is the author of *The Evolutionary Journey of Woman* and an editor of *Integral Voices on Sex, Gender and Sexuality*. She is the chair of board of the South Coast Writers' Centre, and also the founder of The Neo Perennial Press, established as part of Wollongong Council's Creative Spaces program.

Caitlin White, a writer and artist based in Wollongong NSW, is the Submissions Manager and Co-Editor for the Heroines Anthology. They are the editor of *Baby Teeth Journal* and Social Media Manager for Wollongong Writers Festival, as well as a freelance copywriter and blogger.